The Art Forger's Handbook

Eric Hebborn

THE OVERLOOK PRESS

WOODSTOCK • NEW YORK

Other books by Eric Hebborn

Drawn to Trouble: The Forging of an Artist, an Autobiography

This edition first published in paperback in the United States in 2004 by
The Overlook Press, Peter Mayer Publishers, Inc.
Woodstock and New York

WOODSTOCK:
One Overlook Drive
Woodstock, NY 12498
www.overlookpress.com
[For individual orders, bulk and special sales, contact our Woodstock office]

NEW YORK:
141 Wooster Street
New York, NY 10012

By arrangement with Cassell Illustrated, a division of Octopus Publishing Ltd

Library of Congress Cataloging-in-Publication Data

The art forger's handbook / Eric Hebborn
p. cm.
Includes biographical references and index.
1. Art—Forgeries—Handbooks, manuals, etc. I. Title.
N8790.H4 1997   702'.8'74—dc21   9645710 CIP

The ideas and opinions expressed in The Art Forger's Handbook are those of the author and not
the publishers, and their publication does not imply approval or otherwise by the publishers. All
art techniques and practices described in this book are for information only and should not be
undertaken without full regard to their legal consequence. The legal views expressed in this book
are those of an art forger and not a lawyer, and readers should proceed with utmost caution.

Designed by Gwyn Lewis
Special photography by Amanda Heywood
Typeset in Monotype Bell by AccComputing, Castle Cary, Somerset
Printed and bound in Great Britain by Creative Print and Design (Wales), Ebbw Vale

ISBN 1-58567-626-8
3 5 7 9 8 6 4 2 1

Contents

CONTENTS

List of Plates

Preface

Ludovico Arrighi, called Il Vicentino, was the greatest writer of the Renaissance and is one of my heroes. He is known as a connoisseur of calligraphy (which is really a form of drawing) through his famous manual on this subject, *L'Operina*, published in Rome in 1522. In the introduction Arrighi informs the reader that he has undertaken this work because he 'has been asked several times, and supported by many friends'. A lot of people had indeed asked him with great persistence to teach them the art of calligraphy, and, not being able to instruct them all personally, he had the idea of making use of the recent invention of the printing press in order to distribute his knowledge in this field.

More than 400 years later I find myself in an analogous situation. Like Arrighi, I have written a practical manual to satisfy those people wanting to learn an art that seems to appeal to many people: the forging of paintings and drawings. Not a week goes by without people sending me letters or telephoning to ask advice on how to create new 'Old Masters'. It is impossible to answer all these questions personally, so if these pages satisfy some of the questions, I would say that I have achieved my goal.

I would like to thank the editor at Cassell for the faith he has shown in me, and Archeus Fine Art of New Bond Street, for their time, relieving me of my troubles. Without them both, the book would never have been created.

Once more my thoughts coincide with those of Arrighi, who says, in the conclusion of his manual:

> Reader, if you find something that offends you in this treatise by Vicentino,
> do not be upset, because divine and not human is he who has no vices.

E.H.

Introduction

Mundis vult decipi, ergo decipiatur
(The world wants to be deceived, and so it is)

SEBASTIAN FRANCK, *Paradoxa* (1533)

T he story is told of two rival artists in ancient Greece, who, to settle the matter between them as to who was the better painter, agreed to submit a painting each to a panel of experts. The judging took place out of doors, and to protect the pictures from sun and dust they were covered with cloths. When the cloth was removed from the first picture, the judges were amazed at the beauty and realism of the work: a bunch of grapes. As they stood in silent admiration, a flock of birds swooped down and began to peck at the painted fruit. At this one of the judges said: 'Have not these birds decided the matter for us? Is not this picture so beautifully painted that even they are convinced that the grapes are real?'

Even so, the judges thought it only fair to look at the second picture before giving a verdict. Now imagine everybody's surprise when upon trying to remove the cloth from the second work, it was discovered that the cloth itself was in fact painted: a veritable masterpiece of *trompe l'oeil*. Whereupon the judges declared the second painting to be even better than the first, saying, 'The first work has merely deceived an ignorant flock of birds, whereas this second work has fooled some of the finest connoisseurs in the land.'

Apocryphal as this old tale doubtless is, it does suggest that the deceiving of the expert is a time-honoured practice. Fakes, frauds, forgeries and hoaxes involving works of art would seem to be almost as old as art itself. A drawing of a bison's head on a stone discovered in a cave in Spain is thought by some scholars to be either a study for, or a copy after, or an imitation of a similar drawing on the walls of another cave; nobody can be quite sure.

Nevertheless the question of attribution is a relatively modern one. It would seem that authorship was not of much interest to early man and what mattered to him was the work itself. Although pure conjecture, art was not perhaps so much admired as required for magical purposes, functioning independently of its makers. Certainly such an attitude to art survived into the early civilizations. The Sumerians, the Egyptians, the Babylonians and the ancient artists of both India and China have left us countless master-pieces, all anonymous, and scarcely one that could be called original in the sense that it reflects one person's individual, unique point of view. The artist–craftsman of those times was content to set aside his ego and follow accepted models that speak of cultures rather than idiosyncrasies. Their works conform to Virginia Woolf's definition of a masterpiece. 'Master-pieces', she says, 'are not single and solitary births, they are the outcome of many years of thinking in common, of thinking by the body of the people, so that the experience of the mass is behind the single voice.'

It is not till we come to the world of ancient Greece that the names of a few artists are known to us, either from them having signed their works or being mentioned in classical texts. And no sooner was the practice of signing works of art introduced than forgery followed. Curiously, the first of these forgeries were perpetrated by the artists themselves. When, for instance, Phidias, a celebrated sculptor of Athens, wished to help his favourite pupil, Agoracritus, to sell a statue of Aphrodite, he signed the work himself. Similarly, Apelles, the eminent painter of Kos, is said to have signed and offered for sale certain works by Protogenes.

The practice of famous artists lending their names to promote the work of their less distinguished followers has continued down the ages. In the eighteenth century the fashionable French painter François Boucher (1703–70) signed copies made by his pupils. In the nineteenth century another French painter, Ingres (1780–1867), signed a copy made by his pupil Amaury-Duval (1808–85). Corot (1796–1875) was notorious for the practice – and in our own time Picasso (1881–1973) said: 'If the counterfeit were a good one, I should be delighted. I'd sit down straight away and sign it.'

The artist clearly has a different attitude towards the 'authentic' and the 'spurious' than the dealer, expert and collector. Sir Osbert Sitwell tells this anecdote about the painter Walter Sickert (1860–1942).

I recollect with what apparent delight he [Sickert] related to me how his eye had been attracted to a certain picture in the window of a shop in the neighbourhood of Holborn. He was on the other side of the road, but the vaguely familiar aspect of the canvas caused him to cross to examine it. It was like something he knew and yet different... Then he saw stuck above the picture to the glass of the window a piece of paper. Printed on it in large letters was the name Sickert. When he came nearer, he recognised the canvas as one abandoned when only half completed some years before. Since he had last seen it, it had been beautifully finished and had acquired, with every appearance of verisimilitude, his signature. 'I couldn't have improved on the picture myself,' he said. 'Now I need never finish them any more and often it gives me quite a lot of trouble! I only wish I knew the name of the admirable artist who finishes and signs my things.'[1]

On another occasion when some pictures alleged to be by Sickert's hand were coming up for auction, either a partner in the firm, or an expert who had begun to doubt their authenticity, had telegraphed to him: 'Did you paint the lots signed with your name at present on exhibition in these auction rooms?' Sickert had gone to inspect the pictures and had then wired back: 'No, but none the worse for that. – Sickert.'[2]

We are all aware of the close association in our minds of such words as art and artfulness, craft and craftiness, artefact and artifice. We also speak of the cunning craftsman and use such phrases as 'his hand has not lost its cunning'. All of which tends to suggest that there is a confusion in our minds as to what in the arts and crafts belong to aesthetics and what to ethics, two fields of enquiry that still belong to the diminishing science of philosophy. Indeed it is possible that the origins of our inability to define the boundaries between morality and beauty can be traced to the philosophy of Aristotle, who in his imitative theory holds, roughly speaking, that all art is imitation. Some artists imitate nature, some imitate art, but all artists imitate. From this it follows that should we condemn the imitation of former art as unethical (in our own age, even criminal), we are in the embarrassing position of having to accuse such masters as Michelangelo, Cellini, Rubens, Rembrandt, Fragonard, Delacroix, Degas and hundreds of other distinguished artists who have indulged in the practice as, at the very best, shady characters.

However that may be, it would certainly be presumptuous of me to speak in these pages of matters that have defied a satisfactory analysis by some of the most subtle intellects in history. Instead I shall, as far as possible, avoid any serious mention of beauty or morality and confine myself to an account of the materials and methods of the forger's art. These, with the exception of those involved in ageing techniques, are, of course, precisely the same as those used by the Old Masters themselves. For this reason the following chapters may serve not only the aspiring forger but also the art lover as an introduction to the fascinating field of artists' techniques, for it is only by understanding the painter as a craftsman that we can truly appreciate him as an artist – even though we may go no further than a little armchair forgery.

As many secrets as possible are given away, largely because the analytical chemist makes them quite impossible to keep. Nevertheless, the reader should always bear in mind the famous Chinese saying: 'If the wrong man uses the right means, the right means work in the wrong way.' You should not expect that by studying this book you will at once turn out fabulous fakes, amaze your friends and confound the experts.

This observation brings me to an important point, and one that should be made at the outset. Throughout this book a distinction is made or implied between the 'perfect' fake and the decorative fake. The author of the 'perfect' fake has set out to make his or her production indistinguishable from the kind of work that they wish to emulate. The maker of the decorative fake makes no such attempt but simply tries to follow more or less closely the style of the chosen master and give the work a pleasing appearance of age. Naturally it is the 'decorative fake' that is more likely to be within the average faker's reach, and consequently I have given many recipes that would be quite unsuitable for pictures intended to pass the scrutiny of the connoisseur and/or the scientific investigator. Even so, the genuine fake has not been neglected, and the book may well be of interest to the professional forger as well as the tiro.

In the space of this volume I can do no more than introduce my subject and hope that its theme will gain your interest and sympathy. Certainly there is no room to speak of how to draw or how to paint, but that is no great loss, for as Max Doerner points out: 'One can as soon learn to draw or paint from a book as you can learn to swim on a sofa.'[3]

In conclusion I would like to recommend this handbook to the student of art history. 'Nothing', says Friedrich Winkler, 'is to apt to sharpen one's ability to discern the genuine as the recognition of the false.'[4] And who better equipped to recognize the false than a practised forger? It was not only the artists of the past who learnt from making copies and imitations – so did those interested in becoming connoisseurs, and I feel strongly that the practice should be revived. By augmenting their normal studies by practising for themselves the techniques of the Old Masters, the student could not fail to gain a deeper knowledge of their subject than a solely scholarly or academic approach allows. The Italian writer and diplomat Baldassare Castiglione (1478–1529), in his manual for courtiers, *Il Cortegiano*, instructs the sixteenth-century gentleman as to those things he should know, among them the art of painting, saying: 'Even if this art affords you no pleasure, it will give you a better understanding of things and a clearer appreciation of the excellency of ancient and modern statues, vases, monuments, medals, cameos, carvings and other such objects.'[5]

To such good counsel I can add nothing, except to say, do as I do and forge ahead.

PART ONE

Old Master Drawings

Dates for the Introduction of Drawing Materials

Prehistory Charcoal

Lamp black, or candle black

Black, white and red chalk

Antiquity Watercolour known to the Egyptians as a dyestuff

AD 100 Chinese invent paper

795 Paper-mills established in Baghdad

1270 First Italian papers (Fabriano)

1336 First paper-mills erected in Germany

c.1390 Cennini gives instructions for making a lead pencil

1400 Black, white and red chalks are used extensively from the fifteenth century onward

1496 First English papers

c.1500 Watercolours introduced (said to have been invented by Dürer)

1586 First paper-mill in Holland

c.1700 Pastel had a great flowering in the eighteenth century

1755 Introduction of wove paper. Before this date all hand-made paper was made on a laid mould

1790 First modern pencil (graphite)

1798 Machine-made papers in long lengths

1831 Gillot patented an example of a steel pen nib

1880 Wood fibres and starch incorporated into papers

1930 Up to 100 per cent chemical fibres used in paper-making

CHAPTER ONE

The Devil's Kitchen

'God sends meat – the devil sends cooks.'

CHARLES VI

Art forgers are commonly believed to operate from dens. Nothing could be further from the truth. The successful forger usually works in the same kind of well-lit studio as his more reputable colleagues, the painter and the restorer. This book is not, however, written for the successful forger whose skills have given them the means to rent or buy a proper studio but for the beginner, who may be obliged to cultivate his or her nefarious talents in some odd corner of their own home where the light is good. This may, of course, be the attic, the bedroom, the living-room or wheresoever, but here I am going to make a special case for the kitchen.

The arts of drawing and painting have long been associated with the culinary arts. The frequent mention of sugar, honey, glycerine, eggs, milk, cheese, etc. makes the reading of some of the old painting manuals as appetizing as that of a good cookery book, which they closely resemble. For example, the Italian artist and writer Cennino Cennini (1365–1440), writing in the early fifteenth century, goes as far as to suggest that panel paintings themselves indulge in something akin to eating and drinking.

> Do you know the effects of the first glue? A weak water is absorbed from it
> by the wood, which operates exactly as if when fasting, you eat a few comfits
> and drink a glass of wine, which gives you an appetite for dinner; so this
> glue prepares the wood for the glue grounds to be applied afterwards.[6]

In his book *Collecting: An Unruly Passion*, Dr Werner Muensterberger, a practising psychoanalyst, argues that 'the taste for finer things seems to begin in the mouth and then wanders to the eyes'. He then quotes the distinguished connoisseur of master drawings, Paul Sachs, as saying: 'Anyone who professes an interest in the fine arts and is indifferent to the joys of the palate is automatically suspect.'[7]

However that may be, I am not suggesting that you work in or near the kitchen in order to stimulate your aesthetic sensibilities with frequent raids on the food cupboard. No, the reason is that cooking, like painting or drawing, is not only an art but also a craft, and many of the tools and materials employed by the cook are equally useful to the maker of new Old Masters. The following list should make this clear.

The kitchen sink

Water is used in innumerable processes involved with the faker's art: processes including the bleaching, tinting, stretching and flattening of paper, the preparation of inks, pastes and glues and the cleaning of the brushes, to mention those that first come to mind.

Eggs

Egg is, of course, used in the process of painting known as egg tempera, which has a tradition behind it centuries older than that of oil painting.

Milk

Milk can make a useful fixative for pencil, chalk and pastel drawings.

Bread

Breadcrumbs may be used as an eraser and for reducing the darkness of chalk drawings to simulate the rubbed look so often found on old drawings.

Potato

A half of a potato rubbed over a grease-stain on paper will normally permit one to draw over the area with ink, which would not otherwise take on it.

Coffee, tea and chicory

These may all be used for the tinting of papers.

Olive oil

Olive oil may sometimes be the cause of interesting stains.

Gelatine
Gelatine can be used as a glue or size in certain processes.

Flour
For making pastes.

Pastry-board
Pastry-boards are made in the same manner and can be put to the same use as drawing-boards. On the whole they are of better quality than drawing-boards to be found in the art shop.

Ice trays
In his memoir *The Fake's Progress*,[8] the well-known forger Tom Keating (1917–84) tells us that he prepared his tints of sepia ink for the 'Samuel Palmers' in an ice tray, filling each compartment with a different shade ranging from light to dark.

The kitchen stove
A source of heat is necessary for many of the forger's activities, the preparing of certain pastes, glues and oils as well as the hardening and cracking of oil paint.

This list of tools and materials that may be of service to the ingenious forger and which can be found in a reasonably well-fitted and stocked kitchen is very far from being complete, and, as will be shown below, the pestle and mortar, the kitchen scales and the cutlery, plates, bleach and detergents may all be brought into play. As, of course, may be the kitchen table (especially if it has a marble top). Nor should the humble dustbin be neglected for the disposal of our failures, for as the Italians say: '*Non tutte le ciambelle riescono con bucho*' ('not all doughnuts come out with holes'). A culinary version of our English proverb: 'Not all our ducklings turn into swans.'

But however well equipped your kitchen may be, it is most unlikely to contain all that you will need for the artistic concoctions it is your aim to produce, and the following two chapters are devoted to a discussion of the papers, inks and drawing instruments that are not normally at hand and where or how to obtain them.

In passing I would like to mention the only bulky piece of equipment the forger may find useful: a standing screw press, variously described as an office copying press, nipping press or bookbinder's press. You might well find such an article in a junk shop. The bed of a press of this sort will measure anywhere from 25×50cm (10×20in) to 50×40cm (20×15in). The larger it is, the more useful it is. It would, however, only be worth buying one very cheaply because one can flatten one's 'Old Master' drawing equally well under the weight of a pile of cookbooks, and one can print one's collector's marks with a spoon.

CHAPTER TWO

If All the World Were Paper

Rags make paper

Paper makes money

Money makes banks

Banks make loans

Loans make beggars

Beggars make rags

ANONYMOUS

The first business of the forger of Old Master drawings is to collect a stock of period paper. But before I direct you to the principal sources, it is necessary for you to know both what you are looking for and what you are looking at. A sound knowledge of paper used in the past is a must, and the crucial thing you should know about it is how it was made.

Hand-made Paper

The following delightful and accurate account is given by the seventeenth-century English diarist John Evelyn (1641–1706).

I went to see my lord of St Albsaans house at Byflete, an olde large building. Thence to the paper mills, where I found them making a coarse white paper. They cull the raggs, which are linnen, for white paper, wollen for brown, then they stamp them in troughs to a papp with pestles or hammers like the powder-mills, then they put it into a vessell of water, in which they dip a frame closely wyred with a wyre as small as a haire, and as close as a weaver's reed; on this they take up the papp, the superflous water draining thro' the wyre; this they dextrously turning, shake out like a pancake on a

9

smooth board between two pieces of flannell, then presse it between a greate presse, the flannell sucking out the moisture; then taking it out they ply and dry it on strings as they dry linnen in the laundry; then dip it in alum-water, lastly polish and make it up into quires. They put some gum in the water in which they macerate the raggs. The mark we find on the sheets is formed in the wyre.[9]

For greater clarity, here is a description of the process in modern English. The paper is made of linen and other rags of strong fibre, which are thoroughly beaten up into a thin soup with water. The sheets of paper are made one at a time by the vatman who, taking up a rectangular sieve the size of the sheet to be made, dips it into the fibrous soup. His sieve, which has a very fine wire mesh at the bottom, is known as a mould. When he has run off the excess water from the mould, the vatman holds it level and gives it a shake. His skill is such that he can keep the mould so level that there is never more than one-thousandth-of-an-inch variation in the thickness of a sheet from one end to the other. This done, the wooden frame of the mould (the deckle) is removed and the wet soft sheet shaken off the wire mesh on to a felt blanket. Another piece of felt is placed on top, and alternating sheets and felts are stacked up to form a pile known as a post. The post is then put into a press, and after pressing the sheets are dried and matured in lofts before being sized by passing them through a bath of glue (size). The toughness of any given sheet depends on the quality of the rags, the strength of the size and the amount of pressure applied.

The important thing for the faker to remember about all this is that the vatman shakes the mould in more than one direction with the result that the fibres do not all lie the same way, head to tail as it were, as we find in machine-made paper. Consequently hand-made paper does not have a grain. It is easy to distinguish the fine parallel lines of the wiremarks on hand-made sheets from the grain of machine-made paper.

Watermarks

Watermarks are formed by making the design in wire and attaching it to the mesh at the bottom of the mould. The mark, being higher than the mesh, causes the paper to be thinner along its lines, and in consequence the mark becomes visible when the sheet is held up to the light. These designs used by paper manufacturers as trademarks have proved very useful to the scholar in the dating and localizing of drawings, but experts are perfectly aware that even when a mark actually contains a date it can rarely give anything more than a *post quem* indication of when the drawing on it was in fact made. This being so, don't imagine for a moment that a watermark of the right date for the master you are following is a passport for your work's acceptance. Naturally, the decorative fake may have any watermark whatever. Some of the marks are in themselves highly decorative. A few examples are given below, and we shall be returning to them in a later chapter dealing with the forger's library.

Forging watermarks

Although I do not recommend it, watermarks can be so closely imitated as almost to defy detection. The plan adopted is to procure paper of the desired age and paint the chosen mark on to it with a colourless oil, such as poppy oil. Another method is to scratch the design into the back of the sheet with a razor-blade or scalpel. This must, of course, be done with the utmost nicety and skill, so that when some over-curious person holds the paper up to the light to examine the mark with a magnifying glass they will find the paper in that area neither too rough nor too smooth as to possess an unnatural gloss. Excessive roughness can sometimes be corrected by passing a hot iron over it, whereas unwanted gloss may be removed by slightly damping the area and delicately roughening the surface with a stiff but flexible brush.

Machine-made paper

All papers were made by hand until the very end of the eighteenth century when, in 1798, a paper-making machine was invented in France by Louis Robert. A little before that, experiments had been made in the manufacture of sheets from wood and other fibres. With the development of these new materials and techniques much cheaper paper became possible, which gradually replaced the hand-made product for all but the most important work. Papers made of wood pulp are, however, inferior in every way to rag paper: they are weaker, more inclined to discolour and less pleasing both to eye and hand. For these reasons those of us who wish to give our customers a fair deal will have little to do with them. True, there are various methods of producing a chemical wood-pulp, and these are all superior to the mechanically produced item (which is little more than sawdust); a certain amount of hand-made rag paper is produced to this day. But, nevertheless, if we are to succeed in our endeavour to emulate the draughtsmen of the past we must use the materials that they themselves used and go in search of the genuine article.

Where to find old paper?

The best places for handling genuine old sheets of paper prior to buying them are: the saleroom, where you can rummage through the unframed lots of prints and drawings; the print-seller, who has similar folders of unframed pictures, and the antiquarian bookseller, where you may find the end-papers of his books more interesting than what lies between them. Another place you must frequent to learn about paper is the museum, but unless you happen to have the necessary qualifications, you may have to content yourself with looking at the prints, drawings and books it may have on show through glass.

Books are particularly useful to the beginner because the date and place of publication are normally to be found on the title page, and these more often than not indicate the date and provenance of the paper on which it is printed. Prints are also useful in this way but to a lesser degree. For instance, one may be looking at a perfectly genuine etching by Rembrandt (1606–69), which is signed and dated 1645, and one might suppose that the paper is Dutch, seventeenth century, only to discover later that it is a posthumous printing of the master's plate, printed as late as the nineteenth century and in England. I shall say nothing of drawings in this respect, for, as we all know, the right artist and the right paper may not meet for centuries.

Only when you feel confident that you can judge with a fair amount of accuracy the date and quality of any given sheet should you start to collect. You have already met your three principal suppliers, that is the saleroom, the print-seller and the bookseller.

The saleroom

The majority of people who attend an auction of Old Master drawings are after quality – the best they can afford. Or else they are looking for a find, which is, of course, still being on the look-out for quality. We forgers, on the other hand, while not being indifferent to the virtues of fine draughts-manship, are much more interested in bad drawings than good ones. Draw-ings of no more worth than the paper on which they are drawn. Perhaps these wretched scribbles are so slight as to be scarcely visible, in which case we may be able to help; or the draughtsman has modestly left empty the back of his bad drawing, awaiting an abler hand to fill in the blank.

Then we should consider the good sheets of period paper on which the bad old drawings may be stuck down. Or, perhaps, they are in nice period mounts, bearing fascinating inscriptions or illustrious collector's marks. Surely such mounts deserve to be recycled, especially in our ecologically conscious time. Here you must show imagination when deciding on what to bid. Naturally, whenever funds and opportunity allow, you should bid on good, albeit minor, drawings by a master draughtsman to keep for study. The smaller auction houses are those most likely to have what you are looking for but keep an eye on them all. One day you may have the pleasure of spotting one of your own efforts among the works of quality.

The print-seller

As a rule the dealer in prints does not have much to offer us beyond the pleasure of looking through his stock. What he may have, however, are large, not too important or expensive old prints on very thick paper. These may be split in half (*see* p.18 for splitting process), thus providing a large sheet of period paper without damaging the print; which may if one wishes be sold to cut costs. Should you make friends with the print dealer, you may well discover in his back room things that have more interest for you than for him. To give an example: the G. B. Piranesi (1720–78) drawing (*see* plate 3) is drawn on genuine eighteenth-century paper that actually has the watermark of a paper used by Piranesi himself. This was made possible by a print-seller friend of mine who had acquired some Piranesi etchings in their original bindings, and as his profit lay in selling the prints separately, he dismantled the books and discarded the bindings together with the end-papers and a number of sheets, which I was, of course, happy to purchase.

The bookseller
You should frequent second-hand booksellers of all kinds, from the antiquarian of good address to the proprietor of a stall in the flea market; for it sometimes happens that they have in stock whole volumes of blank or partially blank paper in the form of unlined ledgers or account-books. These may frequently be dated virtually to the year by the first entry. Mostly they come from the eighteenth and nineteenth centuries, and naturally the further one goes back in time the harder it is to find them. If the bookseller in the flea market has any old volumes at all, they are most likely to be in a pitiful condition, totally beyond repair, and yet some part of them may still be useful. These carcasses have two advantages for us. The first is that they should cost a pittance. The second is that we may dismember them without qualms. That is, soak off any paper there may be on the boards, salvage any end-papers, cut away margins and so on, all with a clear conscience.

This brings me to an important point – we are fakers not vandals, creators not destroyers. Therefore, when collecting material for our creations, we show respect for the work of former artists and would as soon tear out a page of a beautiful book as scrape off some paint from a Rembrandt. Whether the bookseller has anything of interest to you in stock or otherwise, tell him what it is that you are looking for, and he may very well be kind enough to put such material as comes his way aside for your next visit. Buying a book for your bookshelf is the best way of getting the dealer on your side in this matter, for as the old adage goes: 'Nothing links man to man like the frequent passage of money.'

Preparing old paper for drawing

Let us assume that you have been fortunate in your search for old paper and now have a pile of it and perhaps a ledger or two and are anxious to begin to draw. Before you can start, however, the paper will normally require treatment. This may not be the case if you intend to draw in pencil or chalk, but it is invariably so if ink or watercolour are to be employed. This is because the old glue in the sheet will have disintegrated, leaving it exactly like blotting-paper; should you draw with ink upon it, your lines will bleed, that is spread out – something connoisseurs are quick to notice.

Apart from putting back some glue into the old sheets, there are other things that may have to be attended to before drawing can begin. It is a common mistake among forgers to 'age' the paper they use for their fakes. Nothing could be more ridiculous, because if the paper is genuinely old it needs no ageing, and if it is not old it should not be used (except of course for decorative work). But if it needs no ageing, it may require a little cleaning and repairing if it is to be transformed into an 'old' drawing that has survived the vicissitudes of time in a good enough condition to at least be legible. Instructions are given below for carrying out such cleaning and mending operations as may from time to time be found necessary.

Repairing worm-holes

This operation is necessary to prevent the draughtsman from covering the inside edges of the holes with tell-tale ink. The repair is removed when the drawing is complete.

Prepare some pulped paper – the simplest way is to chew it. Lay the sheet on a marble slab and taking a well-chewed, perfectly soft piece of pulped paper larger than the hole to be mended, place it over the hole. Now place over the pulp several pads of blotting-paper, and then with a small wooden mallet weld in the pulp. Over and over again the cunning craftsman strikes on the surface of his pad. Not heavily but as gently as the circumstance requires, the process being precisely the same as gold-beating. As time goes on the pulp is felt to harden, until at last it practically forms part of the sheet into which it has been impressed. When it is thoroughly dry, the paper that protrudes is cut out or scraped away with a razor-blade. It will be readily understood that the repair of worm-holes is work of a most delicate nature. A great deal depends on the fibre of the paper and much experience is necessary, so avoid it when you can.

Removing grease-spots

When grease-spots occur in awkward places, for example where a face is to be drawn, they should be removed. This should be carried out before any bleaching, tinting, or sizing is undertaken as the presence of grease may interfere with these processes. Lay the sheet down on a smooth, hard surface. Then take some clean blotting-paper or cotton wool and make it into a smooth pad, which is then dipped into benzine and applied to the grease spots. Do not rub the marks but pat them very gently again and again until the spirit amalgamates with the fat and carries it off by evaporation. Another method is to sprinkle the stain with powdered chalk or talcum powder, cover with paper and pass a hot iron over it. A variant is to exchange the chalk or talcum powder for blotting-paper.

Rectifying a greasy surface

A greasy surface will need to be treated if you are to draw on it with ink. It may be freed from grease by rubbing it over with purified oak-gall, dilute ammonia or a peeled and halved potato.

Removing surface dirt

First method. Lay paper in a flat dish and cover with cold water to a depth of about 3mm (⅛in). Expose to the sun's rays for a day or two, and all but fixed stains and dyes will be gone.

Second method. To remove all dirt that is not fixed, cover the paper with strong flour paste. Wash this paste away, and any free dirt on the paper will be washed away with it.

Third method. Finest powdered salt is dissolved in hot lemon juice to form as stiff a paste as possible. This is spread evenly over the surface and left for an hour, after which the paper is washed clean with boiling water. The sheet must then be allowed to dry slowly – never in the sun or before a fire. This dangerous method may only be used on very strong paper.

Bleaching paper

Unsightly stains, or those in awkward places that have survived ordinary washing and one or other of the three cleaning processes given above, may often be removed by bleaching. As the old papers were made out of rag – that is to say, cloth – for this reason they respond to the same bleaching agents as are used in the laundry. These are oxidizing bleaches, such as hydrogen peroxide, which break down the stains into colourless compounds that may then be washed away. In its simplest form the process is undertaken like this:

1. Prepare in a photographic tray of suitable size a mixture of one tablespoon of household bleach to one litre (two pints) of water.
2. Place paper on a sheet of plate-glass to act as a carrier and immerse into the bleaching mixture.
3. Watch closely for any change in the colour of the stain and/or the paper. If after 15 minutes there is no appreciable difference a little more bleach can be added, but remember that if the bleach is used too strong there is the danger of the paper being attacked and weakened. It may also turn the paper a startling white, ill-suited to its age.
4. After bleaching, the paper must be washed in running water for at least 15 minutes.

Should you wish to be more scientific about it, reach for your white coat, rent a laboratory and proceed as follows:

It is assumed that your laboratory has a well-lit fume cupboard furnished with running water, a drain and a window for observing the progress of the operations carried out inside it. You now prepare a solution by adding 75ml (3fl.oz) of 40 per cent formalin to 60g (2oz) of technical sodium chlorite, dissolved in 3 litres (6 pints) of water. The solution will be seen to turn yellow. This is due to the formation of chlorine dioxide, which, like your household bleach, is an oxidizing substance. As in the homespun method given above, the stained paper is laid on glass so that it may be safely handled and is immersed in the bleaching solution that has been poured into a photographic tray. The careful watching of the process, any necessary modification of the bleaching liquid and the thorough washing to remove sodium salts are all as given above.

The advantage of this method, which is employed by professional restorers of prints and drawings, is that it does not turn the paper unnaturally white. Its disadvantage from our point of view, and one it shares with all bleaching processes, is that it removes all those lovely water stains, fox-marks, mildews and fly dirts that if left would speak so forcibly of our future drawing's age. Nevertheless, disfiguring stains should be removed, and bleaching is often the only way of doing it.

Sizing paper

Before sizing you must erase any unwanted inscriptions in pencil, such as booksellers are apt to put on end-papers – an Old Master drawing with '2 vols £10 5s', inscribed on the verso might excite suspicion. If left, the size will fix such writing, and it will be found exceedingly difficult to remove it afterwards.

To prepare the size dissolve 25g (1oz) of gelatine into a litre (2 pints) of water or powdered hide glue at the rate of 175–225g (6–8oz) to the 4 litres (1 gall) of water. Polycell diluted to a milky water may be used for decorative work. The size may be brushed on to the paper or the paper immersed in it. If the paper is very delicate it should be laid on glass and the whole submerged in the size, which has been poured, like the bleach above, into a photographic tray. Very absorbent sheets should be sized two or three times, starting with a weak size and allowing the paper to dry between each sizing (plate 4 illustrates the problems that can arise when sizing is not done properly). Once sized, the sheets should be hung up to dry on a string with clothes pegs or some other clip, otherwise they may stick to whatever surface on which they have been laid.

Tinting paper

If you should have over-bleached a sheet, and it has exchanged the mellow colour of age for a clinical whiteness, you may put matters right by adding some colouring agent to the size. A weak solution of permanganate gives a yellowish tint that matches most old papers, but many other substances such as stout, coffee, tea, chicory and liquorice may be used. To discover if the desired colour has been obtained, a piece of white blotting-paper is dipped into the tinted size, blotted off and dried. Not until the test piece has thoroughly dried will you be able to judge the true colour. The tint is, of course, corrected by adding more water or more stain as required.

Splitting paper

Cover both sides of the paper to be split with a thickish flour paste and then place the sheet between two pieces of strong and finely textured cloth, slightly larger than the paper – linen is the best for this purpose. The whole is ironed on both sides to ensure that the cloths stick firmly all over. The encased paper is then left under the weight of a pile of books until the paste is thoroughly dry, which will be a matter of weeks rather than days. Now you carefully pull apart the two cloths, whereupon you should find half the paper attached to each. The separated cloths, each with a sheet of paper attached to it, must now be put into warm water until the paper floats off. One should only split strong papers and avoid any sheet containing coarse fibres as these are likely to leave holes on one of the resulting sheets with corresponding bumps on the other.

CHAPTER THREE

And All the Sea Were Ink

'Let there be gall enough in thy ink,

though thou write with a goose pen.'

WILLIAM SHAKESPEARE

Having considered the principal support for Old Master drawings, that is paper, we must now turn our attention to materials used for drawing upon it. The first of these is ink. As with the number of pigments employed by the best painters, so with the number of inks used by the best draughtsmen; they are few. This does not mean that practically every liquid capable of making a mark on a surface, from blood to blackberry juice, has not at some time or other been adopted, but experience and tradition have shown that a few inks, tried and true, suffice for virtually all line drawing on paper. They may be divided into four categories: carbon, iron, bistre and sepia.

Ink

Carbon-based ink

Carbon ink is extremely stable. It was used by the ancient Egyptians for writing and drawing on papyrus, wood, potsherd and other materials. This early writing fluid was a mixture of soot suspended in some medium such as oil, gum or glue. The old binding material has long since decayed, but the carbon remains black, and having grown, as it were, to be one with the object upon which it was drawn, it is still in place. Both Chinese and Indian inks are carbon inks, and as they are easily obtainable today and chemically speaking do not differ appreciably from the old carbon inks, they should find a place in the forger's kit. The modern waterproof inks must, however, be avoided as they contain varnish, which glistens in a way quite foreign to old drawings. Furthermore, these varnishes are usually synthetic, and the analytical chemist would have little trouble in identifying them. The best Chinese ink still comes in small sticks from China, but beware of imitations. It is not unknown for European manufacturers to wrap up the inferior sticks of their own making in fine rice-paper covered with alluring Chinese characters in a manner almost worthy of our good selves.

Iron-based ink

Iron ink is compounded from iron and gallotannic acid. The tannins are available from a number of natural sources, the best-known one being the oak-gall. Oak-gall, or iron-gall, ink has been identified on works dating from the second century BC, and it is reasonable to suppose it was in use before this time. It was still in use during the early Middle Ages and was to become the principal ink of the Renaissance; from then on its place was contended for, first by bistre and then by sepia, but it has never entirely gone out of use, and there are still some of us who find employment for it, even today.

Unfortunately, however, iron ink is not generally available in artist-supply shops, and we are obliged to manufacture it ourselves. In the past it was prepared from a multitude of recipes with the result that it appears on old drawings in a wide variety of tints and hues, ranging from a yellow so faded as to be scarcely legible – to a strong black – that might easily be mistaken for a carbon ink. In between are rusty browns and various greenish tints, and quite often more than one of these variations can occur on the same drawing. Another quality of this ink is that due to its acidity (caused by the presence of tannic and sulphuric acid) it may with time eat through the paper. This can, with skill, be nicely imitated to give a most convincing appearance of age.

Below are two basic recipes for iron ink, one old and the other from the nineteenth century, when making gall ink seems to have been a cottage industry. Providing the result is what you want they may be varied more or less as one likes. Personally, I keep the wine of the first recipe for drinking.

RECIPE 1

Put into a quart of water two ounces of right gumme Arabik, five ounces of galles and three of copras. Let it stay covered in the warme sunne and so it will prove good incke. To boyle the sayd stuffe together a little upon the fire would make it more speedy for writing: but ye unboyled yeldeth a fayrer glosse and longer endureth. In stead of water wine were best for this purpose. Refresh your incke with wine or vinegar when it wareth thicke.

Francis Clement: *Petite Schole* (1587)

RECIPE 2

1. Leave 125g (5oz) of finely powdered gall to soak for three days in two litres (4 pints) of rain-water.
2. Dissolve 50g (2oz) of gum arabic and 50g (2oz) of iron sulphate in a litre (2 pints) of rain-water.
3. Mix the two solutions together and leave the mixture to stand for a few days, stirring occasionally.
4. Bring ink to the boil.
5. Strain through fine muslin and bottle.

Incidentally, if you have no luck finding oak-galls on your country outings, acorns that have been left to rot a little under the trees will do almost as well. The galls, or acorns, may be crushed in your kitchen mortar.

Bistre

Bistre is made from the soot resulting from burning beech, pine or willow logs that is suspended in rain-water, in which gum arabic has been dissolved. It was very much used in the seventeenth and eighteenth centuries and is particularly beautiful in the hands of a master who knows how to lay washes. Such masters as Rembrandt, Nicolas Poussin (1593/4–1665) and Claude Lorrain (1604/5–82) managed to achieve a marvellous luminosity with it. Unfortunately it is a difficult colour to find in commerce, and the making of it, at least from my own experience, is seldom satisfactory. Doubtless there is a good method known to the old inkmakers, but so far I have not discovered an entirely satisfactory recipe. Sometimes one comes across it in old paint-boxes, and if one should, it is worth paying a good price for it, even though you may have to buy the whole box just for this one colour. An excellent surrogate is raw umber, made up as watercolour in a tube. Buy a good make, and it is virtually indistinguishable. It is, of course, diluted with water until the desired strength is obtained. Its colour can be modified to match any particular example of old bistre by the addition of other earth colours such as raw sienna or burnt umber, both of which are chemically acceptable for our purposes.

Sepia

This ink, principally made from the dye of the cuttlefish, did not come into general use until the late eighteenth century, and those drawings by seventeenth-century masters that are so frequently described by experts as being in sepia are more often than not in bistre. As with carbon inks, sepia is still easily obtainable from the art shops; there is no need to go fishing – but here again you must avoid the shiny waterproof varieties with their false glisten. Sepia in the form of good-quality watercolour is perfectly acceptable, providing the binding material is gum arabic. This is because new and old gum arabic in the minute quantities that may be removed from a drawing for testing react to scientific analysis in much the same way.

Drawing Instruments

The pens of the Old Masters were the quill and the reed pen, and these in the hands of the best practitioners produce qualities difficult to emulate with any other kind of pen. A look through the drawings of Rembrandt is particularly instructive on this point. Of all draughtsmen this artist had a profound feeling for his tools, and when he draws with the reed he allows his pen to speak its own language and produce lines that only a reed pen can produce. It is the same with his use of the quill, the brush and the chalk. He never forces them out of character, although he is always in control of the situation; he is like a good composer who exploits the nature of his instruments, never letting one do the work of another and getting the best out of them all.

The quill

The quill is made from the pinion feathers of birds. First find an amenable bird. To cut a quill one requires a very sharp penknife or scalpel and a small cutting-board or slab. The process is described by Edward Johnston in his classic writing manual, *Writing & Illuminating & Lettering*,[10] from which the following explanatory drawings have been taken.

1. Strip off the barbs of the feather.

2. Shorten the shaft to a convenient length.

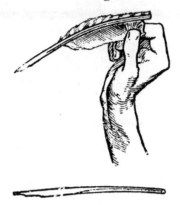

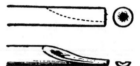

3. Make two cuts at the drawing end of the quill, the first like this:

and the second like this:

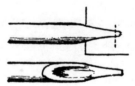

4. Lay the quill facing upwards on the cutting-board and make a clean cut to shape the drawing tip, either straight across like this:

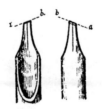

or at an angle like this:

Johnston recommends making a reservoir for the ink and gives the following diagram:

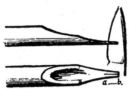

Personally, I have never found this necessary. It may save one having to dip one's pen into the ink as frequently, but labour-saving is not a serious consideration for the artist, for seldom is his time money.

5. The tip of the quill is slit and opened like this:

The reed
The reed is cut in much the same way as the quill, for which Johnston's preceding explanatory drawings suffice.

The metal pen
Metal pens have existed since Roman times, but it was not until the nineteenth century that they were made sufficiently flexible to be used for drawing. Even for writing they were considered more as prized possessions than as handy tools. Their status in the eighteenth century can be judged by a comment made by Parson Woodford set down in 1790: 'This wrote with a copper pen, late my mother's.'

The person who did most to popularize the steel pen was an unlettered button manufacturer from Birmingham called Joseph Gillot, who in later life was nicknamed 'his Nibs'. This ingenious man discovered that he could apply certain techniques used in the making of buttons to the manufacture of flexible steel nibs and patented an example in 1831. People were quick to realize the two main advantages of the new tool. It came ready shaped and was easy to control, and these virtues spelt the end of the long era dominated by the quill and the reed as drawing and writing instruments. As may be judged from the advertisement below, which appeared in the illustrated catalogue of the International Exhibition, London, of 1862, the early steel nibs were delightfully ornate.

REPRESENTATIONS OF STEEL PENS.

AS MADE BY

C. BRANDAUER & CO.

Manufacturers of Steel Pens of every description,

NEW JOHN STREET PEN WORKS,

BIRMINGHAM.

Such nibs are also functional, and stripped of their ornament they still serve those of us who prefer to wield tools than press buttons. They are easily obtained, and you should lay in a stock of various widths.

The brush

Brushes for brush drawing must be of the finest quality. Sable watercolour brushes are excellent, but these are absurdly expensive. Fortunately for our pocket, technology has made a perfectly good substitute for them, and synthetic 'sable' brushes are available at a fraction of the cost.

Brush drawing in Europe has never enjoyed the esteem in which it is held in the Orient. Essentially our Old Masters took to the technique for a specific purpose. Pure brush drawing, that is to say without being combined with the use of the pen, dates from the seventeenth century, when artists were preoccupied with the representation of chiaroscuro and reflected light. Brush drawing is ideal for rapidly setting down these things. The wash is applied with the brush in such a way as to leave untouched areas of paper to stand for the light passages. Splendid examples of European brush drawing are to be found in certain passages of Rembrandt's line-and-wash drawings, a number of Poussin and Claude drawings, where the brush alone is used, and in Tiepolo (*see* plates 5 and 6). Manet also used the technique wonderfully well, as did Picasso, but these last are far too recent for our attention.

Stick

If, for instance, the handle of a brush is sharpened to a point and used like a pen, it gives a very agreeable line, similar to those found in certain Old Master drawings. I have used it myself in the making of sketches in the styles of various eighteenth-century masters such as Reynolds, Romney and Rowlandson. It has some of the force of the reed pen, and in the right hands and given its head it may produce some happy accidents. Just as it may, in the wrong hands, produce some unhappy ones.

Silverpoint

Metal points of various kinds were known to the Romans and were probably used for writing on parchment. An instrument with a point of lead, or an alloy of lead and tin, was used for drawing in the fifteenth and sixteenth centuries in preparation for a finished drawing in other materials such as pen and ink or black chalk, much as we might use a lead (properly graphite) pencil for an underdrawing today. Sometimes the indentations made by this ancestor of our pencil can be detected under the final work. Rarely was this lead point used for drawings in their final form, and the preferred metal point for finished drawings in the early and high Renaissance was silverpoint.

Silverpoint scarcely makes a mark on unprepared paper, and this led to Italian artists almost exclusively confined to Florence and Umbria (the technique was unknown in Venice) to invent what we call Carta Tinta, or tinted grounds, composed of powdered bones mixed with gum water, Chinese white and whatever pigment was needed to give the desired colour. White chalk was sometimes used in place of the Chinese white, and this may be the best course to follow. The reason being that Chinese white is a form of white lead, and unless one prepares the pigment oneself (*see* p.100) one is likely to be using a modern form that differs slightly from the traditional product in its chemical structure and can be identified by X-ray diffraction. For practice and decorative work there is nothing wrong with the Chinese white as bought off the shelf. Another useful surface to practise on is modern art paper of the kind used for glossy magazines.

Before turning to the preparation of old paper for silverpoint, let us take a look at the point itself. Ideally what is required is a length of silver wire as used by jewellers. This should be about the thickness of the 'lead' in a pencil and an inch or so in length. This is mounted into the holder that etchers use for their etching needles and that can be found in any well-stocked art suppliers. Failing this you may use any silver object that happens to have or can be given a point. For many years my own silverpoint consisted of the handle of an old silver teaspoon that had been brought to a point at its narrow end. It was with this spoon-handle that I made a drawing with something of a chequered history.

It was a study of a curly-headed young man on a pink ground highlighted with Chinese white and resembling the work of Lorenzo di Credi (c.1458–1537), one of the greatest masters of silverpoint. A photograph of the drawing was shown by a prospective customer to the late Sir Anthony Blunt, the distinguished art historian who was Surveyor of the Queen's Pictures (1945–72) and Director of the Courtauld Institute of Art (1947–74). The would-be-buyer had mentioned to Anthony, whom I knew personally, that the drawing had been offered to him by myself. This led Anthony to tell me his opinion of it, based on the photograph; it was totally negative. He found it coarse and unpleasantly harsh in its contrast between the lights and the darks, and very much doubted its authenticity.

It happened that I was staying with him in London, so without bothering to comment on his opinion I casually left the drawing on the mantelpiece in my room, where he came across it. The change in Anthony's attitude was dramatic. The 'unpleasant harshness' was transmuted into 'a pervasive gentleness', the young man's beauty was extolled, and Anthony's former misjudgement put down to the poor photograph that had distorted the contrasts of tone. Nevertheless he was cautious enough to ask me if he might have the drawing examined by the Courtauld's scientific department. I agreed to this, and the drawing came back to me described as 'undoubtedly old'. More than this, Anthony had got in touch with Ellis Waterhouse, later Sir Ellis Waterhouse, then Director of the Barber Institute of Fine Art in Birmingham, suggesting that he might purchase the work for his museum. Waterhouse was as enraptured by the piece as Anthony, but was not able to raise the funds – thus sparing the Barber Institute from much later embarrassment. I nevertheless found a buyer in a highly important dealer in Old Masters called Hans Calmann, who sold it to one of his wealthy clients for an undisclosed sum with a firm attribution to Credi.

Encouraged by this success, I thought I might make another drawing in the same vein and offer it directly to Calmann. Now this was a very risky thing to do. Silverpoint drawings from the Renaissance are extremely rare, and for two of them to turn up in rapid succession, both on pink paper heightened with white and both of handsome youths, was bound to raise suspicion. Unless, well, unless the drawings when put side by side were so clearly by different masters, with their own idiosyncrasies, that no connection between them other than their age and type existed. To this end I prepared the pink ground of my second drawing according to a different recipe and applied it more thinly to the period paper, which also came from another batch, this time with a watermark that dated it to *c.*1425. It also seemed prudent to exchange my spoon-handle for the prong of a silver fork. These things attended to, I made another drawing of 'pervasive gentleness', which on this occasion Calmann gave to the workshop of Verrocchio (*c.*1423–88). A few years later the first of these drawings came back on to the market, where it fetched a low price on account of 'unfounded' rumours concerning its authenticity. Ten more years went by, and again it turned up at auction. Some time in between some idiot had set about 'ageing' it; it was so battered that I scarcely recognized it, and its poor condition led to an even poorer price. Such was this particular fake's progress.

But to return, literally, to the point – the silverpoint. It should be finely rounded but not sharp, otherwise it will scratch and tear the paper. It wears relatively little with use. The line it produces is of a very light silver-grey tone, which soon becomes brownish through oxidation. Dark lines are obtained by working over the same place several times. Shaded areas are best worked up with fine parallel lines in the manner of Leonardo, who was in fact the strongest influence on Lorenzo di Credi's style. The painter and biographer of artists, Giorgio Vasari (1511–78) has this to say on the subject:

> As Lorenzo was inordinately fond of Leonardo's manner, he learned to imitate it so well that no one could excel him in rendering Leonardo's precise and careful finish. This is evident in numerous drawings in my possession, among them studies made from soft clay models draped with sized canvas and reproduced with incredible, inimitable care and patience.[11]

The silverpoint line is indelible, making corrections by erasure impossible.

As mentioned above, silverpoint scarcely marks ordinary paper, and in order to force it to deposit the silver, the paper must have an abrasive ground. Here is a recipe for laying such a ground by Cennino Cennini, to whose *Il libro dell'arte* the reader is directed for further recipes:

When you want to tint a kid parchment, or a sheet of paper, take as much as half a nut of terre-verte, a little ocher [*sic*], half as much as that; and solid white lead to the amount of half the ocher and as much as a bean of bone dust, using the bone which I described to you for drawing (*see below*) and as much as half a bean of vermilion, and grind up all these things well on the porphyry slab with well or spring or river water; and grind them as much as ever you can stand grinding them, for they can never be done too much, because the more you grind them, the more perfect tint it becomes. Then temper the aforesaid substances with size of the following quantity and strength: get a leaf of druggist's glue, not fish glue, and put it into a pipkin to soak for the space of six hours in as much clear, clean water as two common goblets will hold. Then put this pipkin on the fire to temper it and skim it when it boils. When it has boiled a little so that you can see that the glue has all dissolved, strain twice. Then take a large paint pot big enough for these ground colours and put in enough of this size to make it flow freely from the brush. And choose a good-size soft bristle brush. Then take the paper of yours you wish to tint; lay some of this tint evenly over the ground of your paper, running your hand lightly, with the brush about half dry, first in one direction and then in the other. And put on three or four coats of it in this way, or five, until you see the paper is tinted evenly. And wait long enough between one coat and the next for each coat to dry. And if you see it shrivel from your tinting, or horny from the tinting mixture, it is a sign that the tempera is too strong, and so, while you are laying the first coat, remedy this. How? Put in some clear, warm water; when it is dry and done, take a penknife and rub lightly over the tinted sheet with the blade, so as to remedy any little roughness that there may be on it.[12]

Preparation of 'Carta Tinta'

Cennini offers his own advice on how to prepare the bone dust necessary for this production process.

You must know what bone is good. Take bone from the second joints and wings of fowl, or of capon; and the older they are the better. Just as you find them under the dining table, put them into the fire; and when you see that they have turned whiter than ashes, draw them out, and grind them well on the porphyry and use it as I say above.[13]

But here is a simplified version of Cennini's method of preparing Carta Tinta:

1. Take three heaped tablespoons of finely ground white lead (this can be bought already in powder form from a reliable colourman, otherwise you have to prepare it yourself), and add to one heaped tablespoon of powdered bone.
2. Dissolve a little gelatine into a cup of hot water to make a weak size. Test strength by taking some between the thumb and forefinger. As it dries it should become slightly tacky, but no effort should be necessary to separate the thumb and finger.
3. Add the size water to the white lead and bone, stirring it to form an easy-flowing creamy mix. Add to this mix any colouring required, using only earth colours such as terre vertes, the umbers, ochres and siennas (*see* plate 7). If blue is wanted, you must use pure ultramarine, that is lapis lazuli, or else a bluish tint can be got with lamp black.
4. Put this mixture into a small saucepan, and bring very slowly to the boil, stirring occasionally. Remove from heat at once.
5. When the mixture has cooled, take a flat brush of fine bristle about 5cm (2in) wide, and brush the mixture at least twice over the paper, which should be taped to a board all round the edges so that it will dry flat. The mixture may be thinned with water as necessary.

If your size was too strong your drawing surface will have an undesirable gloss. This may sometimes be removed by suspending it above a steaming kettle, and when thoroughly dry, rubbing it lightly with the finest possible sandpaper. Cennino Cennini's use of a knife to remove roughness should only be necessary if you have failed to powder the bone sufficiently.

Charcoal, Chalk and Pastel
Charcoal
Charcoal is one of the very oldest materials for drawing. It was used by early

man and seems to have found employment ever since. Literary sources tell us that it was used in Greek times; scribbles in charcoal have been discovered on the walls of houses in Pompeii, and many modern artists still use it. The best variety is made from willow- or lime-wood. It can be bought with no difficulty, but should you happen to be an inveterate do-it-yourselfer, here is how.

Take a tin can complete with lid and, using a nail or other pointed instrument, pierce numerous holes into the top and bottom of it. Pack the can loosely with willow-twigs and slim boughs and put it all into the middle of a very big bonfire. This is a great excuse for you to have a picnic party with your friends or family – you need not tell them that just as good charcoal (if not better) is for sale in your local art-suppliers. The party must go on for hours and hours until the great fire is burnt out, at which point you can safely recover your tin of charcoal from the ashes and merrily go on your way. The greatest master of drawing in charcoal from the technical point of view is the German painter and engraver Albrecht Dürer (1471–1528). Somebody may prove me wrong one day, but I believe his magnificent charcoal portraits are truly inimitable – and I imagine that I am not the only one to have tried and, it must be admitted, failed to make one.

Chalk

The English critic, novelist and poet G. K. Chesterton tells the story in his essay 'Chalk' of how he once went sketching in southern England. He liked to draw in coloured chalks on brown wrapping-paper, and in spite of his landlady considering him somewhat eccentric to want wrapping-paper with nothing to wrap in it he had managed to persuade her to give him a sheet, which he had taken with a box of chalks to make a sketch from the cliffs overlooking the English Channel. On arrival he discovered that he had used up his most important chalk – the white one. This caused him to curse himself quietly for his forgetfulness and prepare to go back to town to buy a stick or two from the stationers, when all of sudden he burst into a fit of laughter because he realized that he was sitting on countless tons of white chalk. All he had to do was pull up a little turf and cut out what he needed.

The technique of à trois crayons

This story reminds us of from where some of our finest pigments, stamped with a brand name and bought off the shelves, really come. Chalk is found in nature as an earth of various colours. The varieties of earth most used for the manufacture of coloured chalks and crayons are black argillite and red chalk. The three chalks so far mentioned – the white, the black and red – are virtually the only ones used by the Old Masters. They have been known and used in various ways since the age of the cave painters. The combination of these three colours is a particularly felicitous one, and we see them constantly reappearing in periods of great draughtsmanship. It was virtually the whole palette of Apelles and Nicomachus of ancient Greece; and, with or without the white, the colours of the ancient red- or black-figure vases. It was much used in the Renaissance; later it was a favourite with Rubens (1577–1640) and through his influence had a marvellous flowering in France during the eighteenth century where Jean-Antoine Watteau (1684–1721) (*see* plate 8), François Boucher and others did such admirable work that the combination of red, black and white chalk has come to be known throughout the world as the technique of *à trois crayons*. A technique that implies the use of a toned paper, otherwise the white would not show up.

It is seldom that one can discover why one combination of colours is more satisfactory than another. Usually it is put down to a matter of personal taste and the threadbare Latin phrase trotted out: *de gustibus non est disputandum*. But, in this case, I believe that there is a semi-scientific reason why the *à trois crayons* combination is a particularly happy one. It has to do with the artist's and the viewer's sensibility to the temperature of light. Painters may sometimes be heard to speak of warm and cool colours. The warmest colours are said to be the reds and the oranges, and the coolest the blues and purples. Now, as we all know, sunlight is our principal source of heat. We also know that this light may be refracted through a prism to divide it into the spectrum, or the colours of the rainbow, and when we do so the painter's warm and cool colours lie at opposite ends of the spectrum. What is intriguing, however, is that if the refracted light is made to fall on to a row of thermometers, those at each end of the spectrum will give different readings. The thermometer at the red end will show a higher temperature than the one at the violet end. In short, what the painter knows by instinct can be demonstrated to have its foundation in observable fact. But what, one may ask, has this got to do with the attractiveness of our technique *à trois crayons*?

Before I can answer this question, we must look briefly at colour. In our sensation of any particular colour we judge it to possess certain properties in relation to other colours. Two of the most important of these properties are: tone, by which we judge a colour to be lighter or darker than the colours surrounding it, and hue, by which we judge it to be yellower, redder, bluer, etc. As far as tone is concerned, our black and white chalks are, in combination, able to find a tonal equivalent for any given colour; just as a black and white photograph does. They are powerless, however, to find a parallel for the said colour's hue. This is because, although we may speak of relatively warm blacks and whites, both colours are essentially cool colours and when mixed together produce cool greys, some of which can be very close to blue. Thus it is that they can only find thermal equivalents or parallels for colours in the cool end of the spectrum. It is only when we bring into play our red chalk from the opposite, warm end of the spectrum that, by combining the three chalks, we can find a parallel for any particular colour's temperature relative to its fellows. With black, white and red, we have the means of conveying both the tonal and the thermal relationships between hues, so giving the viewer a vicarious experience of full colour. It is this power that, albeit acting subconsciously, makes the technique *à trois crayons* so agreeable.

Natural chalks are easily obtainable and are, of course, exactly the same in their chemical structures as those used by the Old Masters or, for that matter, prehistoric man. They are conveniently made up into sticks or pencils. The only snag is that they are forced to keep bad company and are surrounded by hosts of vulgar newcomers on most art-suppliers' shelves; the gaudiest crowd you can imagine, a chromatic nightmare. Some of these modern chalks, those of a more discreet colour, might possibly be mistaken for natural earths by a beginner, so if in doubt go to a reputable colourman and make it clear that you want the natural variety.

Pastels

A kind of pastel technique was used in a number of the cave paintings. In the grottoes of Eyzies-de-Tabac and Font-de-Gaume in France, red ochre has been found in the form of triangular fragments, some of which have been sharpened to a point. Some are long, like pencils, others have holes so that they can be hung up or hung round the neck. Leonardo is supposed to have experimented with pastel, but no drawing in this medium and certainly by him is now known.

Federico Barocci (*c.*1528–1612) made many chalk drawings that approach the quality of pastel. But pastel proper did not really come into its own until the eighteenth century, notably in France, and then one would really call the result pastel paintings rather than drawings. The distinction between the two is this: in a drawing the contours of shapes or forms are made with a line – they are literally delineated – whereas in painting contours are created by the meeting of two or more areas of different tone or colour. Degas (1834–1917) is perhaps the most famous exponent of pastel drawing. But whether you are going to draw or paint with your pastels – a matter that will depend on the master you wish to follow – you are advised to make your own. This is because many of the pastels of the trade are made from fugitive coal-tar dyes, which rapidly fade on exposure to the light. A simple test to discover whether this is the case or not is to dip the pastel into pure alcohol; if the alcohol takes on any of the colour then a coal-tar or another dye is present.

HOW TO MAKE PASTELS

Pastels are made from finely ground pigments mixed with a little binding medium. The pigments (which should be selected from those used for the forger's palette given on pp. 99–103) are ground into a stiff paste with water to which the binding medium is added.

The following binding mediums may be used:

Gum arabic 2 per cent in relation to the quantity of pigment. To this is added a little honey to prevent the sticks becoming too brittle.
Glue or gelatine 3 per cent at the most in relation to the quantity of pigment.
Skimmed milk This is used in place of water; it is a very weak binding medium. Thin soapy water, hydromel and thinned tempera emulsions are similarly used.
Gum tragacanth This is particularly recommended. The tragacanth may be given a preliminary soaking in alcohol. Take 3g (⅛oz) and soak it in a litre (2 pints) of water until it forms a jelly. This is warmed until the tragacanth has the consistency of paste.

Many other binders or adhesives are used, including wax emulsions, much diluted Polycell and even strained oatmeal broth. You will need to experiment to find out what suits you and your pigments best.

When preparing pastel shades, clay, whiting, gypsum or talcum powder are sometimes mixed with the coloured pigments in the place of white. The clay and gypsum must be as finely powdered as possible and pure white. But, according to A. J. Pernety (1775),[14] white lead was employed by the masters of his time. When the pigment and binder have been made up into a coloured paste or dough, this is left to dry a little until it is easy to mould. This may be hastened by laying the mix on blotting-paper or a porous terracotta tile. The dough is then shaped into little balls, and these are rolled out to form the cylindrical sticks for drawing. It is wise to make one test-piece to be sure that you have the right quantity of binding material. This sample is dried in the sun or in an oven. It is then tested on a suitable paper, the preparation of which is given below. It should also be tested with water, for if it is not readily absorbent, this is a sign that the binder is too strong. If all is well, then the rest of the batch is laid out on newspaper or blotting-paper and dried in a moderate heat.

If, however, the stick of pastel is too hard, then the whole mix should be washed by mixing it with water, and leaving it to stand until any excess water may be poured off. A little skimmed milk is added next, and the process of shaping the sticks is carried out as before. But, alternatively, if the test-piece is too crumbly, then a little more binding medium must be added to the paste. It is not essential that your home-made pastels be uniformly shaped, and you will be amazed at the beauty, depth and brilliance of their colour compared to the shop varieties.

PREPARING PAPER FOR PASTEL

A slight texture or roughness of the paper is desirable, but avoid excessive roughness as it tends to 'sandpaper' the pastel and make work difficult. Paper that is too smooth may be treated as follows:

1. Cover surface with flour paste (*see* p. 58), smoothly and without brushmarks.
2. Sprinkle evenly with the finest possible powdered pumice-stone.
3. Shake the sheet to remove any excess pumice powder.

Most pastel drawings are on tinted paper, and you may not have any in your stock of old paper. If this is the case you may tint the old paper with pigment during the sizing process, or mix colour with the surface paste. Do not try to tint unsized paper as unsightly blotches will result. Blotches that, like acne, speak more of youth than of age.

FIXATIVES FOR PASTEL

Pastel drawings and paintings are extremely fragile unless fixed. Quite apart from them being easily smudged, a simple knock can cause particles of pigment to fall off. This means, of course, that fixing pastel is a necessity but an unfortunate one because much of the charm and brilliance of the colour can easily be destroyed by fixing. The first rule is to fix as lightly as possible. The fixative is applied by blowing through a mouth-sprayer, which can be bought or improvised with a straw that is almost cut through the middle and bent so that the two halves form a right angle; one half is then put into the bottle of fixative, and the operator blows through the other half (*see* plate 1). One must be careful not to stand too close to the drawing and first blow into space, then only for a second on the picture. The process is repeated once or twice as necessary. Some formulas for fixative are:

1. 2 per cent mastic resin dissolved in ether.
2. 5 per cent white shellac and 5 per cent Venice turpentine in 90 per cent pure alcohol.
3. 2 per cent white dammar dissolved in benzene.
4. 10 per cent sandarac dissolved in alcohol.

Skimmed milk may also be used, and fixatives already made up in aerosol spray-cans may be employed for decorative work.

CHAPTER FOUR

Old Masters in the Making

'Genius lies not in having new ideas, but being possessed by the
idea that what has already been said is not yet enough.'

EUGÈNE DELACROIX

A t this point it will be assumed that you have procured and prepared old paper, gathered your pens, inks, chalks and so on and are about to choose a master whose manner you intend to follow. Should you happen to possess psychic powers, then it could be that the master will choose you. This is what happened to Tom Keating. An Old Master whom he would call 'the gaffer', Rembrandt, Goya, Degas or whoever it might be, would 'come down' to him, take possession of his body and painting equipment, and pictures would paint themselves. He awoke one morning to find a Goya self-portrait on his easel in place of the painting he had been working on the night before. This is all very well, but there is a snag. When these 'gaffers' come down they generally leave their genius upstairs, and death has so rusted their dexterity that it would really be better for everybody concerned if they stayed where they were. In any case we can get on perfectly well without them.

Should you be interested in going beyond the making of a decorative fake, your period paper may itself suggest an artist to you. This was, for instance, the case with the 'Piranesi' drawing of my making, which entered the Statens Museum for Kunst, Copenhagen, where for many years it was accepted as a work by the master and gave rise to a number of learned catalogue entries (*see* plate 3).

In 1968–9 I had bought a number of large sheets of heavy eighteenth-century paper from a print-seller located off Tottenham Court Road in central London. The sheets were of excellent quality and in first-class condition. Because of this it seemed a pity to cut them down to make a number of small drawings; consequently I had to think of an eighteenth-century artist who sometimes drew on a large scale. As intimated above, the size and texture of the sheets were exactly those used by Piranesi for printing exceptionally large etchings, and as I studied the virgin sheets I thought how splendid it would be to have a magic wand to wave over them and turn them into a pile of preparatory drawings by the famous etcher. Alas, magic wands have been as thin on the ground in my life as the spirits of dead masters, and there was nothing for it but to get down to work.

There are many good reasons for letting the paper choose the master, not least among them is the confidence this inspires in the expert used to handling originals. When, for instance, in the seventies, the National Gallery of Canada, Ottawa, was informed that a number of drawings it had purchased in the belief that they were by the seventeenth-century draughtsman and etcher Stefano della Bella (1610–64), had the unenviable provenance of myself, the curator of Prints and Drawings could not at first believe that the works were modern. One of the principal arguments she used in defending the drawings and upholding the attribution to Stefano was that the paper on which the one was drawn was identical to that of an undoubtedly genuine drawing in the Louvre. She was quoted in a newspaper at the time as saying that 'the two sheets appear to have come from the same batch'. This saved my drawings from being downgraded for a few more months.

A disadvantage of allowing the paper to decide the master for you is that it sometimes happens that the artist to whom it points is not one with whom you feel happy. If this is the case, and you don't happen to like, let us say Piranesi, then those lovely sheets had better remain virgin. For it is a matter of importance that you feel the utmost admiration and reverence for the master you are to follow. Without these feelings you can never hope to produce good work. An attitude close to veneration is our greatest asset. This gives us a sense of our own integrity as an interpreter, or a copyist, based both on modesty and self-respect. In this we resemble the good translator. Like them we are content to act as if we are only artisans, not perhaps as pure in heart as the anonymous craftsmen who built so many of the world's wonders from pyramids to cathedrals but, nevertheless, like them serving with simple and single-minded devotion, a beauty for which we personally take no credit. My bottom line here is: choose an artist you truly admire.

My little sermon over, we come to another snag. You may adore Leonardo, Michelangelo and Rembrandt, but if, as is almost certainly the case, your adoration far exceeds your abilities, it would be wise to cultivate an admiration for some of the minor masters. You must continually be looking at original drawings of all kinds and collecting as many reproductions of them as you can afford. Peruse these regularly so that you know them, as it were, 'by heart'. Gradually you will find yourself developing an eye for that ineffable thing in them we call quality, and you will find it not only in the works of illustrious artists but also in those of many little masters as well. These artists are so numerous there is little point in mentioning any particular names here. You must simply look and look.

How the experts sometimes choose artists to fit certain pictures was told to me by the late Harry Ward Bailey who was for some time Christie's representative in Rome. When cataloguing a number of pictures for a sale of minor paintings there are usually a number of pictures whose authorship can only be guessed at, and in these cases the method of guessing has been known to be this. A number of authorities gather together, each having a volume of E. Bénézit's monumental *Dictionnaire des peintres, sculpteurs, dessinateurs et graveurs* (*Dictionary of Painters, Sculptors, Drawers and Engravers*) (1960). They close their eyes, each opens their volume at random and points to a name. Names are compared and the most likely one adopted. Although this method is of no use to us in choosing a master to follow, it may be useful in making an attribution for a decorative fake where no particular artist has been imitated.

Deciding on What Kind of Drawing to Make

You may imagine that having chosen a master you have at the same time decided on what kind of drawing you are going to make. This is not necessarily the case, for the same artist will draw in different ways according to the purpose for which his drawing was made. Nowadays we tend to view drawings as autonomous works of art whose object is to please, but this was not the way the Old Masters saw them. That anybody other than a fellow draughtsman would bother to hang up a drawing for admiration would have seemed ludicrous to artists for whom a drawing was simply a means to an end. It was part of the process of producing a complete work of art in another medium: a building, a statue, a painting or whatever.

For this reason the style of any given Old Master drawing does not depend so much on taste as on purpose. We often hear people expressing their views about drawings and saying such things as, 'I like the freedom of this drawing,' or 'it is too slight,' or, again, 'it is too laboured,' thus praising or damning a work with no idea why the artist was one day drawing freely and another day labouring at his work. Certainly the Old Masters were not working with the tastes of the twentieth century in mind. Style and purpose to them were intimately linked. Thus an artist working towards, let us say, an easel painting or a mural might make a number of drawings in different styles. He might start with rapid sketches in pen and ink to work out the general composition, make careful studies from a model for details of the design and then make a highly finished modello to show his patron what the finished work would look like. Or again he might produce a full-sized drawing or cartoon (the word comes from *cartone*, Italian for heavy paper) from small finished drawings and make the enlargement by squaring, that is by ruling the same number of perpendicular and horizontal lines on the small drawing as on the same-proportioned larger paper intended for the cartoon and so facilitate a proportional enlargement. Sketches, studies, modelli and cartoons by the same artist might very well be totally different in technique and drawing style. A clear example is that of the Bolognese painter, Il Guercino (1591–1666) who has two quite distinct drawing styles, one a closely worked chalk technique for making studies from life and the other a free rapid line-and-wash style for working out his compositions (*see* plates 9 and 10).

So before you start, ask yourself why the master you are following might have made such a drawing. One has to follow not only the hand of your chosen artist but also the workings of his mind. A drawing is a reflection of the draughtsman's thought processes. As Michelangelo wrote in *Rime*:

> Pen and ink can show me no preference
> for low or high or mediocre style
> and marble may be fashioned rich or vile,
> to match the sculptor's own intelligence.[15]

At this point let us turn to the workings of the mind of a great draughtsman and see how it might suggest to us a new drawing in his manner. The artist whose thoughts we shall attempt to follow is Rembrandt. Like all good draughtsmen, he was not an isolated talent but a link, a golden one, in the long chain of traditional draughtsmanship that began with our earliest ancestors and is only now becoming anachronistic and threatened with extinction. Because of our twentieth-century concern with originality we tend to see the very great artists of the past such as, for example, Pieter Brueghel the Elder (*c.*1525–69) and Rembrandt, as totally different – two unique artistic personalities with no connection between them whatsoever. This is due to the fact that time has obscured their links. What we see is analogous to the tips of two icebergs whose sunken parts are one, both being parts of a vast continent made up of minor artists, who, though having failed to emerge as distinct peaks themselves, nevertheless provide the foundation without which our giants could not exist..

One of the many artists upon whom Brueghel's drawing style rests is Hans Leonard Schaufelein (*c.*1483–1538). The copy of one of this master's drawings (*see* plate 17) was made for the purpose of getting to know Brueghel's manner before undertaking my version of his much-copied work, *The Painter and the Connoisseur* (*see* plates 11–16). Brueghel was not the only artist to benefit from such works as this drawing by Schaufelein: a look at the drawing of a lady (*see* plate 18) by Hans Holbein the Younger (1497/8–1543) shows a number of resemblances that speak of some connection between them, perhaps a common source of influence, or perhaps Holbein actually knew Schaufelein's drawing.

Essentially what we are looking at is an artistic form. These two ladies in their long gowns are following a form that would seem to have been invented by the Greeks. The motif is a female figure whose action is conveyed by the movement of her garments; any number of variations could be made on this theme, but a certain constant must exist if the work is to be successful. First the figure must be shown either in profile, or near profile, so that her drapes can be seen extending behind her, to describe the space through which she has passed, thus introducing the time element without which action is impossible. Second, she must not be foreshortened, because this stunts the movement. And, third, her drapes must be in some kind of motion; they cannot just hang down as if on a peg. These rules are as strict as those imposed on the writer of a sonnet and can only be broken at the expense of the form.

As it happens Rembrandt actually owned Holbein's drawing, which it seems formed part of the master's large collection of prints and drawings kept in two volumes. One is intriguingly described in an inventory of 1656 as containing drawings by 'the principal masters of the whole world', and the other as being 'full of curious miniature drawings as well as many woodcuts and prints of all kinds of costumes'. Rembrandt was not only a great artist but also a connoisseur and, to get to know Holbein's drawing in a way that I would highly recommend to the connoisseurs of today, he made a copy of it (*see* plate 19). Once having copied it, the forms became part of his store of images that he could draw from freely using his memory alone.

Rembrandt was one of those artists who continually took what he wanted from other artists to use for his own ends. So thoroughly did he absorb motifs from his sources that when we see him quoting from another's work, unless we are as thoroughly acquainted with the original as he was, we simply take it for his own invention. Indeed, it is always totally Rembrandtesque. He was the kind of fully fledged artist that Lionel Trilling had in mind when he wrote: 'The immature artist imitates. The mature artist steals.'

For instance, Holbein's influence lies behind the vividly natural drawing of *Saskia Carrying Rumbartus Downstairs* (*see* plate 20), of which I have made a copy (*see* plate 21). The rapidly drawn lines convey such a sense of immediacy, and every detail of this domestic scene is so marvellously observed that one cannot help but feel that the artist must have drawn it from life. But a little reflection shows that this could hardly have been the case. His wife is seen walking downstairs, her feet moving from one step to the next in a way that would be impossible for a model to hold. The dress, too, is in motion, and moving fabric cannot easily be made to freeze. Furthermore, Saskia is on what is clearly a narrow flight of stairs, and the draughtsman would have been obliged to be either above her or below her to make his drawing. But she is seen from the side, and there is no foreshortening. Doubtless the artist was very familiar with this scene, but he could not have drawn it from life. What we have is a stupendous feat of visual memory combined with a vast knowledge of art in an inseparable, seamless unity. That Holbein's drawing played its part in this creation is made clear by the use of the tassel (or perhaps it is a purse) that hangs down from Saskia's waist to give the essential vertical that speaks of the force of gravity, giving weight to the child and explaining the shift in balance from one of the mother's feet to the other as she descends the steps. The Holbein also has the tassel, indeed it has two and for the same purpose. Rembrandt has Saskia's long gown lifted by the steps, but as he draws the folds from memory it is a mixture of what he saw in Holbein and what he saw in real life.

Holbein's drawing was used more obviously on another occasion by the Dutch artist when composing a picture of Lot being led by two angels from the city of Sodom. On this occasion the whole composition is based on the work of another artist – Rubens (1577–1640). Rembrandt knew the design from a copy of an engraving made after Rubens' original painting by Lucas Vosterman (1595–1675). Thus Rembrandt was working from a copy of a copy, getting his impulse third-hand. Nor was Rubens being original, and the figure of the woman carrying the bundle is, in fact, derived from an engraving by Giorgio Ghisi (1520–82), after a composition by Francesco de'Rossi Salviati (1510–53), who may have taken it from Botticelli (1445–1510). As I have intimated, the figure can be traced back to antiquity. Rembrandt, Rubens, Salviati and the many other artists who have made variations on this theme show their originality and inventiveness not by ignoring tradition but by so thoroughly mastering it that they can use it as though it were something new. Again it is a similar thing to writing. 'Instead of forming new words,' said Horace in *Ars Poetica*, 'I recommend to you any kind of artful management by which you are able to give value to old ones.'

Having seen two instances of how Rembrandt used his knowledge of Holbein's drawing, we may note something curious about his copy of the work. In both his drawings influenced by it the lifted drapery is an important factor. In the drawing of his wife coming downstairs carrying the baby, it is caught up by the steps, thus describing them. In the drawing of Lot leaving Sodom the woman's skirt is raised by her hand, as in the original. Curiously, in Rembrandt's copy he has not drawn the lower part of the figure with this all-important drapery. We cannot know exactly why but let us suppose we invent an explanation. Imagine that he had already made a copy (now lost) of the whole figure, but for some reason or other he was not entirely happy with the upper half and had decided to re-study that part on another sheet (the extant drawing), thus postulating a lost drawing that we might set about 'finding'. We have all the necessary elements for doing so. The former existence of at least two other drawings could similarly be postulated on the evidence provided by our little study. One a copy, or adaptation of Salviati's figure by Rubens; the other a version of Rembrandt's compositional drawing, showing an intermediary stage between his design and that of Rubens, where Lot, for example, might still be shown looking behind him as in the source.

Combining Elements from a Different Original (Pastiche)
Another popular method used by fakers to provide a subject is to combine elements from different originals. This requires much skill if the work is not

to look like a patchwork, as such borrowings are easily spotted by people acquainted with the original artists, and I can only recommend it for decorative fakes. Plate 25 shows one of my own efforts at combining different elements from Leonardo da Vinci (1452–1519) in order to produce a decorative Leonardoesque drawing. The two sources for this work are the bust in a drawing in red chalk now in the collection of the Royal Library, Windsor (*see* plate 23) and the hand from the painting of a *Lady with an Ermine* in the National Museum, Krakow (*see* plate 24). Neither of these two sources is in pen and ink, and the change of medium helps both to unify the elements and to make immediate recognition of the sources more difficult. As I say, I do not really recommend it.

What has been said about copies, variations, translations and so on all presupposes a certain amount of ability to draw, which the reader may or may not possess. Should it be that you have no ability in this field, do not despair but take heart from this story of Jupp Jenniches. Jenniches was a simple-minded museum attendant in Cologne. In 1947 he was sitting in on a large exhibition of works entitled *From Nolde to Klee*, when he overheard certain comments by visitors that caught his imagination. Some of these remarks were derogatory such as, 'Any kid of five could do better.' Others were full of praise by people who thought the works were 'very moving'. During his hours of attendance he studied the pictures on view and came to the conclusion that in spite of not being able to draw, he was quite capable of producing 'very moving' work along the same lines himself. So the very next day saw him turning up to work with a roll of tracing-paper under his arm. Soon he had taken the outlines of a number of pictures, and taking these home he transferred them to drawing-paper, coloured them in and boldly forged the signatures of Nolde, Klee and other artists. This done, he forged certificates of authentication and sold his productions to a shady character, a certain painter, collector and dealer called Schuppner, who previously had been convicted of receiving stolen goods. Schuppner paid Jenniches a reasonable sum for the pictures, and a flourishing little trade began that earned our enterprising museum attendant enough money to rebuild his home, which had suffered from bombing during the war.

All might have continued to go well if it were not for the suspicions aroused by one of the 'Nolde' drawings, which on being shown to the master himself was dismissed as not being his work. At this point Jenniches and Schuppner faced criminal charges, something we should all try to avoid (more of which later). In the event neither man went to prison. Schuppner was found not guilty of persistent fraud and falsification on the grounds of insufficient proof. Jenniches, though found guilty of the same charge and sentenced to one year's imprisonment, was told his sentence would not be imposed providing he remained on good behaviour for the next three years. The court and the public at large were highly amused that a simple man of no education and, more important still, no training or special aptitude for drawing was able to use a roll of tracing-paper to such good effect. Well, what one has done another may do, so if drawing is not your forte, purchase some tracing-paper. A word of warning, however. Old Masters do not lend themselves as readily to tracing as some modern works do, and the non-draughtsman may find it advisable to shift their interest to the twentieth century, where their lack of skill may even prove an asset.

Accessible Artists
So far in this chapter we have mentioned mostly very big names, those of great artists such as Brueghel, Holbein and Rembrandt. We must study the best examples of drawing available if we are to have standards by which to judge our own efforts. In actual practice, however, these great artists are quite unsuitable for the faker's purpose. In the first place they set levels of attainment far beyond our humble talents. Furthermore, even if we did happen to possess the extraordinary abilities necessary to emulate such artists, the experts hum and hah so much about newly discovered works with important names attached to them that even genuine drawings are often rejected. What has happened in the case of most great draughtsmen is that scholars have made a complete catalogue of their known drawings, a catalogue raisonné, that they are very reluctant to add to. And once a drawing has been rejected, no matter how fine it may be, its monetary value is much lower than for a far worse drawing in the manner of a less important artist.

So if you really want to draw in the style of a great master, after having studied his finest drawings, take a look at those of his pupils and followers, to which latter group you yourself rightly belong. Thus in the case of Rembrandt you might try to make drawings in the various styles of his followers who have, in many cases, absorbed the style of the master so completely that it is often extremely difficult to distinguish their drawings from his own. Drawings with 'old' attributions – to Gerrit Dou (1613–75), Govaert Flinck (1615–60), Ferdinand Bol (1616–80), Jacob Koninck (c.1616–

Plate 1 Equipment collected over many years by the dedicated and advanced forger. A watchful eye kept upon the smaller auction rooms will be rewarded with old paintboxes and brushes, making our cookery chores less essential. Many basic tools can be purchased new, but antique equipment, in the author's experience, instils a beneficially antique frame of mind. Note in particular the muslin pouncing bag, the fixative and mouth sprayer and a particularly useful sixteenth-century book of heraldic emblems – essential for convincing provenance.

Plate 2 A surprising amount of everyday cooking ingredients can be used in the course of the ingenious forger's work. However, a sense of moderation is required for skilful use, with the possible exception of wine. The forger will find constant employment for assorted nut and vegetable oils as well as vinegar, honey, cream and potatoes.

Plate 3 For this drawing by Hebborn in the manner of Piranesi of an *Ancient Roman Port*, the paper employed was genuinely of the eighteenth century and of the type Piranesi himself used. The drawing was sold through a London dealer to the Statens Museum for Kunst in Copenhagen where for many years it was accepted as a work by the master.

Plate 4 An example of uneven and visible sizing, just going to show that even with years of practice 'not all our ducklings turn into swans'.

Eric Hebborn, *Studies of the Virgin and Child*, after Raphael (1483–1520), pen and ink, Archeus Fine Art, London.

Plate 5 Giovanni Domenico Tiepolo (1727–1804), *Nessus Seizing Deianira*, brush and wash, sold at Sotheby's, London in 1996 for £8,625.

Plate 6 This forgery, made for an exhibition of Hebborn's work in 1994, was viewed with some interest by the Old Master Drawings experts of all the major auction houses, who collectively judged it to be a poor representation of Giandomenico's style.

Eric Hebborn, *Nessus Seizing Deianira*, in the manner of Giovanni Domenico Tiepolo (1727–1804), sepia ink and brown wash, Archeus Fine Art, London.

Plate 7 Red-tinted paper made using Cennino Cennini's method of preparing Carta Tinta, a time-consuming but rewarding process, which may help to disguise repeated use of the same paper.

Eric Hebborn, *Study for a Caryatid*, after Il Parmigianino (1503–40), sepia ink and brown wash heightened with white on red-tinted paper, private collection, Germany.

Plate 8 The technique of *à trois crayons*, virtually the only coloured chalk technique used by the Old Masters.

Eric Hebborn, *Studies for a Fête Galante and a Female Head*, in the manner of Jean-Antoine Watteau (1684–1721), red, black and white chalk on buff paper, Archeus Fine Art, London.

Plate 9 The chalk technique of the Old Masters for making studies from life, or in our case the technique which should be used by late followers of the Old Masters for making studies for a living.

Il Guercino (1591–1666), *Study of a Naked Man and Woman*, red chalk on paper, private collection, London.

Plate 10 The free rapid line and wash style used by the Old Masters for working out compositions. Generations of collectors have treasured the vibrant drawings made by the Great Masters at this stage of the creative process. Of all styles of drawing, spontaneous ones are hardest for the forger to emulate convincingly.

Il Guercino (1591–1666), *Landscape with Funeral Procession*, ink and wash, Fitzwilliam Museum, Cambridge.

Plate 11 One of the most copied and influential drawings of the late Renaissance of the Low Countries was this semi-autobiographical drawing of *The Painter and the Connoisseur* by Pieter Brueghel the Elder which demonstrates the need for even established artists to make copies to learn from.

Eric Hebborn, *The Painter and the Connoisseur*, after Pieter Brueghel the Elder (*c.*1525–69), pen and ink, Archeus Fine Art, London.

Plate 12 Pieter Brueghel the Elder (*c.*1525–69), *The Painter and the Connoisseur*, pen and ink, Graphische Sammlung Albertina, Vienna.

Plate 13 Jacob Savery I (1545–1602), *The Painter and the Connoisseur*, pen and ink, private collection, Switzerland.

Plate 14 Georg Hoefnagel (1542–1600), *The Painter and the Connoisseur*, pen and ink, private collection, Austria.

Plate 15 Anonymous, *The Painter and the Connoisseur*, pen and ink, private collection, London.

Plate 16 Anonymous, *The Painter and the Connoisseur*, pen and ink, British Museum, London.

Plate 17 shows a faithful copy of an original drawing by Schaufelein, made by Hebborn. From plate 18 it is reasonable to assume that Holbein had seen and was influenced by Schaufelein's work. Holbein's drawing in turn became part of Rembrandt's own collection. Plate 19 shows Rembrandt's version in his own style.

Plate 17 Eric Hebborn, *A Lady*, in the manner of Hans Leonard Schaufelein (1480–1538/40), pen and ink with wash and heightened with white, private collection, London.

Plate 18 Hans Holbein the Younger (1497/8–1543), *Figure of a Woman in Contemporary Dress (an English Lady)*, pen and ink, Ashmolean Museum, Oxford.

Plate 19 Rembrandt Harmensz. van Rijn (1606–69), *Figure of a Woman in Contemporary Dress (an English Lady)*, after Hans Holbein the Younger (1497/8–1543), pen and ink, Nasjonalgalleriet, Oslo.

Plate 20 The Holbein drawing of plate 18, having once been copied, is remembered in detail by Rembrandt and applied in a variant in a later drawing of a different subject. The tassel on the dress is used as a device to imply downward motion.

Rembrandt Harmensz. van Rijn (1606–69), *Saskia Carrying Rumbartus Downstairs*, pen and wash, Pierpont Morgan Library, New York.

Plate 21 Eric Hebborn, *Saskia Carrying Rumbartus Downstairs*, after Rembrandt Harmensz. van Rijn (1606–69), pen and wash, Archeus Fine Art, London.

Plate 22 Although this drawing was not made on old paper, the ageing given to it has been particularly successful, and the sheet speaks of a long and arduous life. The drawing has been treated to a dramatic and exclusive process reserved only for successful work on modern paper – a kettle of boiling water has been poured over it.

Eric Hebborn, *The Mystic Marriage of St Catherine of Alexandria*, after Luca Cambiaso (1527–85), sepia ink and brown wash, Archeus Fine Art, London.

Combining elements from different drawings by the same master, a technique known as 'pastiche', will not fool a serious scholar for a minute. Recently discovered drawings by Leonardo are uncommon, and references to source drawings such as those illustrated are the first port of call of the suspicious expert. Accept that employment of such a technique will produce a decorative result only.

Plate 23 Leonardo da Vinci (1452–1519), *Study for Madonna of the Yarn-Winder*, Royal Library, Windsor.

Plate 24 Leonardo da Vinci (1452–1519), *Lady with an Ermine*, oil on panel, National Museum, Krakow.

Plate 25 Eric Hebborn, decorative drawing in the style of Leonardo da Vinci (1452–1519), pen and ink, Archeus Fine Art, London.

Plate 26 A drawing pricked for pouncing. The drawing is transferred onto the panel by pouncing or filtering finely powdered charcoal through the perforations by using a bag of muslin, a useful technique, even today.

Attributed to Gianfrancesco Penni (1496–1528), pen and ink with wash heightened with white, *Kneeling Angel*, Teylers Museum, Haarlem.

Plate 27 Eric Hebborn, *Kneeling Angel*, after a drawing attributed to Gianfrancesco Penni (1496–1528), but removing these unsightly pinpricks, pen and ink with wash heightened with white, private collection, London.

1708), Gerbrandt van den Eeckhout (1621–74), Lambert Doomer (1622/3–1700) and Nicolaes Maes (1634–93) – as good as they often were, they are not expected to have all the virtues of the master, and one might possibly be successful in an attempt to emulate them. Incidentally, to the long list of Rembrandt's pupils one modern wit had added Hertz van Rental – you might try him. A look through Bénézit's *Dictionnaire des peintres, sculpteurs, dessinateurs et graveurs* could also be rewarding as it contains thousands of entries, mostly listing minor artists of all schools on which you may wish to model yourself and which, I guarantee, will be far more acceptable to the trade than impossibly big names.

Saleable Subjects

Having chosen a master you must now concern yourself with the subject-matter. The general rule is that the less important the name of the artist, the more attractive must be the subject-matter. We are all of us prone to the attraction of a particular subject. Some of us go all gaga over pictures of animals – cats, dogs and horses being quite irresistible. Others love good-looking nudes, male or female. Children are also very saleable, as are views of Venice. My own weakness is for sailing ships. My love of boats may be traced back to a childhood spent in a town on a tidal estuary, and any picture with a reasonably accurate representation of a sailing vessel goes straight to my heart. All this has got nothing to do with art, but if you want to sell your work it must, perforce, be saleable. Unsaleable objects, such as 'The Descent from the Cross', can only be made commercially viable with the addition of a very good name. If in doubt about the saleability of your subject-matter, ask a dealer for advice.

CHAPTER FIVE

Ageing Gracefully

'Everything that deceives may be said to enchant.'

PLATO

I t is a peculiar characteristic of many human natures that when engaged in any operation involving cleaning, brightening or polishing, like Lady Macbeth, they cannot call a halt. Many such characters go into the field of art 'restoration'. Like most attributes this inordinate love of cleansing has its opposite – a love of soiling and ageing – and there are others who are hypnotically carried away by any operation involving staining, tearing, singeing, crumpling and creasing and various other ways of taking upon themselves the duties of time. Once started on these processes, only sudden death can stop them. Many of these sorts are attracted to the forger's art.

As I have mentioned elsewhere, there is nothing more foolish than to attempt to age paper that is already old. Yet, notwithstanding this obvious truth, there are those who stamp it underfoot, bury it in dirt, pour tea or coffee on it, singe its edges and generally do such terrible violence to it that doubts spring into the expert's mind as to how one single sheet of paper could possibly have been exposed to and survived so many and so varied vicissitudes.

Ageing New Paper

Exception should be made, of course, for any new paper that may be used for decorative fakes. This must necessarily have certain signs of having 'aged', but, even here, we must not be over-zealous. The modern paper used should have as little texture as possible without being shiny. It is the mechanical texture of modern papers that is so uncongenial to both forger and collectors of Old Masters. For this reason the best modern paper for general use is simple cartridge paper. It is of even texture, and when laid down – that is glued or pasted on to another sheet of paper or a board – so that it cannot be held up to the light for examination, its true age is not at once discernible. The tinting of paper has been spoken of above (*see* pp. 30–1). This, and other operations concerned with 'ageing' the paper, should mostly be carried out before making one's drawing. It is a common mistake with forgers to make fresh, clean drawings and then try to give them signs of age afterwards. A far better way is to keep the work looking old right from the beginning. If the sheet is of genuine period paper, this is a good start; if not, make your paper appear old before beginning to draw on it.

Smoking paper
If you have had occasion to clean a piece of paper in order to make a legible drawing upon it, you will now wish to correct the whiteness occasioned by the bleaching process. For this purpose you may use an infusion of tea or coffee as mentioned elsewhere. This will give an appearance of age and is effective enough for all practical purposes, but it does mean that the paper has to be saturated again with water. Where this is undesirable, smoking is a useful alternative. A fire is made of green-wood and the drawing held in the dense smoke that arises from it. The paper will then be evenly tinted all over. The longer the paper is held in the smoke, the darker it will become, and so any degree of grime may be imitated. The smoking of drawings to imitate age was the method employed by Michelangelo who was in the habit of borrowing originals and returning copies. Vasari tells us that:

> He also copied drawings of the old masters so perfectly that his copies could not be distinguished from the originals, since he smoked and tinted the paper to give it an appearance of age. He was often able to keep the originals and return his copies in their stead.[16]

How to fake fox-marks
Fox-marks are frequently the result of damp absorbed from the atmosphere. The extent to which paper is hygroscopic (the elegant word for being moisture-absorbent) may be judged from a calculation made at the British Museum. Dr H. J. Plenderleith, who was for many years in charge of the Museum's Department of Conservation, tells us: 'One thousand tons of books

were calculated to absorb at least 20,000lb of water when the relative humidity of the atmosphere increased from 57 per cent to 63 per cent at 60°F.'[17] Excessive moisture promotes the growth of micro-organisms, for which the size in the paper is an excellent nutrient. These, of course, damage the size, cause staining and give rise to fox-marks in the form of rusty-brown spots caused by the accumulation of iron salts on the damaged areas. Tom Keating tells us he imitated these rust marks by damping the paper and then flicking a teaspoon of Nescafé up in the air and letting the grains fall where they would on the paper: 'as the powder descends, fox-marks appear as if by magic'.[18] I have tried this method and discovered that the paper must only be slightly damp and dried quickly after the coffee powder has been sprinkled on it, otherwise the 'fox-marks' become unsightly blobs.

Another method, one that allows you to put the spots exactly where you wish, is to dampen the paper, and taking up a little raw umber in watercolour, apply it delicately with the point of a pen.

A third method, which has the advantage of encouraging the growth of micro-organisms and gives rise to mildew, is as follows:

1. Scrape rust from a rusty object, such as an old nail, and sprinkle it on to a piece of damp and rotten fabric a little larger than the sheet of paper to be treated.
2. Dampen (not wet) the paper, lay it on the fabric and then lay another piece of rotten cloth on top.
3. Keeping the paper and cloths horizontal, put them into a polythene bag.
4. Seal the bag with tape to make it airtight, and store for a week or so in a warm dark place.

Ageing Inks

What has been said of paper is equally true of ink. Your ink should be of the right chemical composition from the start. If, for instance, you want the ink to appear faded, water it down to produce a washed-out look before you draw with it. Thus once the drawing is complete, the clever forger has no need to do much about giving a convincing appearance of age, because it was drawn to look old from the beginning.

Even so there are one or two things that may be done either to rectify some oversight in the making of the drawing or to imitate some special condition brought on by time. You may, for instance, want to give an appearance of your oak-gall ink having eaten its way through the paper. To do this you must study your drawing, examining it for the places where you have deposited the greatest amount of ink, that is to say the heaviest or thickest lines. For it is there that the ink would be most likely to have consumed the paper. Now you take a quill and sharpen it to as fine a point as you can make (*see* pp. 23–5) and with it go over these thick lines with sulphuric acid (one of the acids in the gall). Make sure you work only in the very centre of the lines, pressing with the quill and moving it sideways, up and down the line, until you feel you have scratched through the ink; the acid should do the rest. To help its action a sheet of blotting-paper may be soaked in boiling water and laid on a thin metal tray. The drawing is placed face upwards in the tray, and the whole held over a source of heat. The acid should be diluted and various strengths tested on a scrap of paper similar to that of the drawing.

Generally a slow biting gives a more convincing result than a quick one, but chance seems to play a large part in this process. After the biting, the drawing is thoroughly rinsed and may be baked, not burnt, in a moderate oven. This should be carried out carefully so as not to appreciably change the paper's colour. It is rather like frying garlic, a moment too long, and it is spoiled, so keep a close watch over it. If successful the paper will be brittle, a condition that often accompanies the attack of gallotannic ink on genuinely old drawings.

Built-in age for ink
An ink can be given an aged look before using it simply by mixing it with the same quantity of undistilled water and leaving it for several weeks to evaporate to its former strength. It will then be slightly granular and under magnification will have the same appearance as many old inks. If too granular for use, add one half of it to normal ink.

Creating an Atmosphere of Age
If our work is to convince it must have a feeling of having a past. That is to say it should show signs of having been through the hands of former collectors and dealers, most of whom, we may assume, took care to protect their property rather than submit it to flame and flood. Three forms of protection for drawings have traditionally been used: pasting them into albums, putting them into mounts for storage in boxes, and framing them.

Let us imagine that a drawing was once pasted or glued into an album, later removed and put into a mount, and later still re-matted and framed. What signs of that history would the drawing be likely to show and how can these signs be simulated?

Well, the most obvious sign of a drawing having once been stuck down is when the work is still attached to a page of an album. This, of course, is very easy for us to imitate. We simply paste our drawing on a blank page taken from an old book. A nice refinement is to show signs of another drawing having once been stuck on the back of the page, and to do this you really do stick a drawing on the back. Wait for a week or so until the 'old' glue, or paste (*see* p. 58 for recipes), has thoroughly hardened, then remove the drawing. There is no need to be over-careful about this procedure. If you should leave a little of the paper of the drawing adhering to the mount, or of the mount to the drawing, it adds a very convincing touch.

Remember that when a drawing that has been stuck down on paper for many years is removed, the area to which it was stuck is usually lighter in tone than that occupied by the drawing. This is easy enough to imitate. Make sure that the paper is well sized, then cover the required area with masking-tape and tint the page with a delicate wash of one or other of the tinting agents given on p.18.

Some old drawings have been so carelessly removed from albums that they have entirely lost their corners. These can either be left missing or neatly restored. Obviously the first of these alternatives is the simplest. Many old drawings have had their corners trimmed to remove any unsightly damage. Why should we not do the same?

One of the indications that a drawing has long been in a mount is that it is framed by a narrow strip of a lighter tone where it was once covered by the old mount. This is nicely imitated by masking the edges with tape and tinting the enclosed area as described above. It is best to do this before the drawing is made, as the wetting involved might cause some of the ink to run.

The exposed area of drawing that has been framed and hung in a strong light might have yellowed more dramatically than a drawing that has been mounted and kept in the darkness of a box or portfolio. Furthermore, the drawn lines themselves might have bleached to some extent. The simulation of these things requires two operations. First mask the edges that we fondly imagine were once covered by an old mount and then bleach the drawing (*see* pp.16–17). Second, rinse off the bleach, and tint the exposed area to the right degree of yellowing.

The natural wear and tear of edges

In the course of time the edges of a sheet of paper become worn. If our sheet has been taken from a book, three of the edges and two of the corners will show such wear and tear. The third edge and its two ends, forming the left-hand corners, having been protected by the binding, will not. Furthermore, there might be the undesirable signs of the pages having been freshly cut or torn. To remedy these matters we try to imitate the appearance of the naturally aged edges. If we are dealing with a torn edge, we must first straighten it up by cutting. The cut edge is then stressed. This can be carried out by laying the edge along that of a table and wearing it down both sides with a razor-blade or fine sandpaper. Finish the process by rubbing the edge between your thumb and forefinger. This is the time that it might be accidentally torn but no more than is necessary to match it with the other edges. You can take a nick out of the two corners with your thumbnail or round them off with the edge of the razor. You might have to adjust the colour of the treated area to complete the operation, but normally this is not necessary.

Mending tears

If you have been over-energetic in your stressing of an edge, you may have caused quite long tears, and these should be neatly mended. The repair will suggest to the viewer that some former owner held the drawing in sufficient esteem to take the trouble to mend it. The operation is very simple. One merely has to unite the torn edges and paste a narrow strip of fine Japanese rice-paper to hold them together at the back. I used this method when drawing *The Mystic Marriage of St Catherine of Alexandria* after Luca Cambiaso (1527–85) (*see* plate 22).

Rubbed surfaces

Old drawings nearly always show some signs of rubbing, even if they have been kept in albums. If they are chalk or pencil drawings they might sometimes be so worn as to be scarcely legible, and such work is not much sought after. So, when you rub down a drawing like this with a soft cloth (an old woollen sock serves admirably) before fixing (*see* pp. 36–7), do so gently, and stop before too much damage is done. Ink drawings also get rubbed, and this may be discreetly simulated by a gentle rubbing with pumice powder or the application of the very finest grade of sandpaper.

Before undertaking any of the above 'ageing' processes be sure to study examples of how genuinely old drawings have aged. This is necessary because time does not only destroy but also creates, producing beauties of tone and patina that are most pleasing to the sensitive eye. As old Father Time's apprentices, we have much to learn from him.

Old Mounts

Mounts can often tell us much about a drawing's history and sometimes even about the correctness or otherwise of an attribution. Because old drawings are nowadays usually removed from their original mounts a number of empty ones do turn up and are very worth while collecting.

The earliest important collector of drawings was Giorgio Vasari. He seems to have collected drawings for the specific purpose of illustrating his celebrated work, *Le vite dei più eccellenti pittori, scultori e architetti* (*Lives of the most eminent Painters, Sculptors and Artists*) (1550 and again in an enlarged edition in 1568). He spoke of his collection as the *Libro di disegni*, which, in fact, seems to have consisted of five large folio volumes into which Vasari mounted his drawings and drew, in ink and wash, elaborate frames around them.[19] These frames are wonderful inventions; the artist never repeated himself, and each was designed especially for a particular drawing. Vasari's collection was a labour of love. It was, however, destined to fall into the hands of vandals in the form of dealers who broke the volumes up for profit, and in 1730 the great French collector P.-J. Mariette (1694–1774) wrote *Les débris de la fameuse collection de dessins du Vasari*. Much of this *débris* was at one time in the possession of another famous French collector P. Crozat (1661–1740), who seems to have dismantled it further, for he was upbraided by the English portrait painter and connoisseur Jonathan Richardson the Elder (1665–1745) who described Crozat's action as 'a sort of sacrilege in the Vertù'.[20] It is most unlikely that you will ever come across an original Vasari mount for sale, but they are worth studying for their type, and they might very well be emulated for their great decorative quality. The largest collection is in the Louvre.

The three other collectors mentioned above, Mariette, Crozat and Richardson, also had distinctive mounts. Mariette was France's most distinguished eighteenth-century collector; his drawings are recognizable by the elegant blue mounts to which they are attached. Crozat's enormous collection was largely absorbed by Mariette's, but some of his drawings survive with his own mounts. These are also blue, and you must study originals in the museum to distinguish them. Richardson's mounts are recognizable by a distinctive series of framing lines, including a band of gold and a band of wash. He used card rather than paper and frequently wrote his attribution below the drawing and added an inscription on the verso. Again you must do your homework and look for originals.

Another interesting type of mount is that of Padre Resta (1635–1714) who, because his attributions have come to be looked on as often either absurd and wilful or downright dishonest, has been dubbed by his modern critics as 'that singular but not unattractive charlatan'.[21] Nevertheless he was a great collector, whose influence on Richardson and his son (who was also a painter) and, through them, later generations of English collectors, was profound. Like Vasari, Resta stored his drawings in books and drew, but with less skill, decorative borders for them.

These volumes, at least 16 in number, suffered the same fate as Vasari's *Libro*: with the exception of the famous *Codice Resta* in the Biblioteca Ambrosiana in Milan they were broken up, and their pages scattered throughout various European collections. One of the people responsible for this was the self-same Richardson who so self-righteously complained of Crozat doing the same thing to Vasari's *Libro*. The *Codice Resta* in Milan has been reproduced in a splendid facsimile,[22] but at the time of writing the publishers are asking 5 million lire for it, so putting it out of the range of the average faker; otherwise it would be an excellent tool for study and reference.

Constantly seeing and handling old mounts is the only sure way to get a real feeling for them. In this, the experts have a great advantage over the faker because many of them work for institutions with great collections, and all students of art history with the right qualifications have access to such collections.

Modern Mounts

Old drawings are frequently remounted, so there is no reason why you should not put your new 'Old Master' in a totally modern mount. If you should do so, make sure to use tasteful colours in keeping with the mellowness of age. Following the styles adopted by a good museum might save some institution the trouble of changing the mount in the event of them buying the work. But be careful to change your style of mounting constantly, otherwise you might just as well sign your work with your own name;

remember mounts speak of provenance. Another thing to bear in mind when attaching a drawing to a new mount is to attach it in such a way so that it may be lifted up by the expert to examine the back of the sheet or admire the watermark. Two folded tabs of sticky tape, one at each of the upper corners, is a common method; equally a length of such tape, folded along its own middle and running along the whole length of the upper margin, which acts as a hinge, is also popular. The practice of entirely sticking or laying down drawings has long gone out of fashion, and in some ways even we should keep abreast of the times. If you have been fortunate in your search for old frames and mounts, these will all help you to create an atmosphere around your work, implying a history or provenance.

In almost every operation involved in combining such old material to make a presentable whole you will discover the need for glue or paste.

Glues

Here you must forgo the clean, practical and easy-to-use adhesives of our time and return to the messy and intractable sticky substances of yore. You will need a double-boiler glue pot and brushes reserved for glueing and pasting, together with a sunny nature.

Parchment glue

Parchment glue has long been in use and was recommended by the medieval monk Theophilus, author of a treatise on the medieval arts and crafts *De Diversis Artibus*, the most important source of information on medieval arts and techniques. An equal advocate is the early Renaissance painter Cennino Cennini in his craftsman's handbook, *Libro dell'arte*, which stands between the medieval and the modern periods in outlook, as well as Watin, 'Varnisher to His Majesty King Louis XV'. Here is Cennini's recipe for parchment glue:

> And there is a glue, which is made...of parchment clippings, which one washes well and leaves to soak [or soften] for one whole day before boiling them. Boil them with clear water until the three parts are reduced to one. And when you have no leaf [joiner's] glue, I want you to use this one for gessoing your panels; for there is no better anywhere.[23]

And another good recipe is this one from Vergnard Riffault:

> Put 1kg [2lb] of parchment scraps into 13.5 litres [3 gallons] of boiling

water. Simmer for about four hours or until the quantity has been reduced to half. Strain through a linen or muslin cloth. Leave to cool, when it should have the consistency of a strong jelly. For medium strength, add 2 litres [4 pints] of water and for feeble strength add up to 8 litres [16 pints].[24]

The preparation of parchment glue has never been simplicity itself, and recently it has become more difficult than ever. Added to the very thorough washing of the parchment and the careful watching of the cooking process to make sure the temperature does not get too high, today we have the problem of getting hold of the parchment clippings. In 1930 Hilaire Hiler was able to write: 'Scraps of parchment may be purchased in any big city from firms which have them on hand as a by-product of lampshades, legal documents or other similar uses. Most artist's supply houses can give you an address or sometimes even procure the parchment clippings for you.'[25]

Well, imitation parchments for lampshades and ordinary paper for legal documents have put an end to all that. Where genuine parchment is available, its cost is prohibitive. The parchment bindings of derelict old books might be used, but they are hard to find in quantity, and, in any case, it would be wiser to keep them for making drawings in the manner of the fourteenth- and fifteenth-century artists. These things considered, you may prefer to use some other glue.

Providing you use glues from natural sources you need not worry yourself about future chemical analyses. This is due to the fact that the analyst will not be looking for the remnants of goats, sheep, fish, etc., but for chemical compounds that have diverse origins in nature. This point is nicely made by J. G. Vibert, himself a chemist:

When the ancient authors speak of oyster shells...deer horn, mother-of-pearl, etc., you will understand they are speaking of carbonate of lime, or which the type is chalk. When they speak of the blood of pigs or other slaughtered animals, of milk, of fresh cheese, of the crust of Swiss cheese, yolk of egg or ground-up insects, all that in principle is casein, fibrin or vitelline – which are all about the same thing. If it is a question of fish bladders, cow's tails, old gloves, still-born goats or sheep's hooves, all that is gelatine.[26]

Hide glue
Hide glue has been used in all periods and is still easily obtainable from

hardware stores in the form of powder, pellets or sheets. To judge its quality, colour is our only guide. Although a light-coloured glue is not necessarily good nor a dark-coloured glue necessarily bad, very light-coloured glues (as distinguished from gelatine) are made from bones and sheep skins, and the glue produced from these materials cannot be compared in strength to that produced from hides. A clear, bright claret colour is the natural colour of hide glue. It is inexpensive, simple to prepare and suits our needs admirably. This is how to prepare it:

1. Put into your double-boiler 500g (1lb) of glue to 1 litre (2 pints) of cold water and leave to stand overnight.
2. Place over a fire to heat, and add more water until the glue has the desired consistency. A thin yet slightly creamy solution is about right as any thicker is difficult to manage; indeed, when cool, it may not flow at all.

Fish glue and rabbit-skin glue may also be bought and prepared in the same way.

Paste glue

In their innocence, not a few collectors of the past stuck down their drawings with the glues described above, but as Cennino Cennini tells us in his recipe for an adhesive liquid given below, a flour-based glue was principally used when working with paper. And this paste glue has certainly done less damage to old drawings than some of the other glues, which, you may be interested to know, sometimes attack the paper and stain right through the drawing.

How to make Flour Paste or Batter

Beginning to work on panel in the name of the Most Holy Trinity, always invoking that name and that of the Glorious Virgin Mary, it is necessary to prepare the ground; that is to say, to start to lay various kinds of size. There is one kind of size which is prepared of cooked batter, and it is good for stationers and maskers who make books and also for pasting sheets of paper one to the other, as well as fastening tin to paper. Sometimes we need it for pasting together sheets for transferring designs by pouncing charcoal through the perforated lines. This paste is made as follows: take a pipkin almost full of clear water; heat it well. When it is almost about to boil, take some well-sifted flour, sprinkling it little by little into the pipkin, stirring constantly with a stick or a spoon. Let it boil and be sure not to make it too thick. Take it out, put it in a bowl; if you don't want it to smell (go bad), add some salt and so use it as you need it.[27]

Kitchen-testing has shown that the result is not crucially affected if one omits the invocation of the Holy Trinity and the Virgin. Here follows a modern recipe, which gives virtually the same result as Cennini's.

Take 100g (4oz) of plain flour and 12.5g (½oz) of powdered alum, and mix together with sufficient cold water to form a thin, smooth paste. Old pastes, like old paper, yellow with age, so it is desirable to add some staining agent to the water or else substitute the water with tea or coffee. After taking care to break up any lumps, add a pint of water, or tea or coffee, and gently heat the mixture in an enamel saucepan. It should be stirred from time to time until it reaches boiling point, when it should be simmered and continually stirred for about five minutes.

This will produce a thick paste, which may be thinned with warm water as required. Naturally, smaller or larger quantities can be made, providing the proportions remain constant. Beat up the paste with a flat stick before use. The reader will be pleased to know that, if carefully used, this paste can produce the most unsightly stains.

In this chapter we have been concerned with giving an appearance of age to our drawings, and, as has been intimated, as much depends on how they are presented as any actual ageing technique such as tearing, staining, etc. For this purpose we have perhaps used old papers and mounts to suggest a background or provenance, and we have taken care to make it look as if the drawing and its mount have shared, at least for some time, the same fate. That is to say, if the old mount is stained in a certain way, the drawing on it will be soiled in a similar manner: we don't want a 'new wine in old bottles' look. We may, if we wish to go further in creating this aura of antiquity, add signatures to our work in what scholars call 'the deceptive hand'. True, most collectors hate false inscriptions but, as Cicero said, only 'on other people's statues' (*Odi falsas inscriptiones staturarum alienarum*).

CHAPTER SIX

What's in a Name?

'Giving a name is indeed a poetic art.'

THOMAS CARLYLE

W ho would deny the power of words: 'In the beginning was the Word,' and of all the words the most powerful, the most magical, are names. In both myth and religion the creator utters the name and by doing so calls forth the creatures, or objects, of his creation. Following his maker the ancient sorcerer also drew on the power of names, and making no clear distinction between words and things fancied that by chant and incantation he might call down rain, summon up the spirits of the dead or commune with the devil.

Signatures

The use and the misuse of names is still everyday magic, and at the extent to which we all use them, we all cast spells. But by far the greater number of us do not cast our spells consciously, let alone competently, and we must consider ourselves mere sorcerer's apprentices, more bewitched than bewitching. Call him what you will, the greatest alchemist, magician or wizard of our time is the publicity man. What awesome magic he employs to get the prospective buyer in his thrall and all by the simple expedient of repeating over and over again the name of the product it is his purpose to sell. He makes sure that we see it in magazines, on television, on billboards, around football fields, on T-shirts; indeed, wherever we turn there is to be seen or heard the ubiquitous name. By such repetition (the chanting of old) the publicity man puts us into a trance where, like our forefathers under the spell of the shaman, we can no longer discriminate between words and things.

At this point, no matter how good the quality of a nameless article may be, we do not buy a watch, a drink or handbag but rather a Rolex, a Coca-Cola, a Fendi or some other magic name.

So it is with drawings and paintings. The art dealer uses precisely the same selling techniques as the merchant trading in other luxury goods. A work with the name of a famous artist attached to it has had a spell cast over it. A spell that, although not necessarily cast by the artist himself, greatly increases its price. Some years ago a story circulated about a wit in Paris who asked the price of a certain drawing, signed and framed, that was hung in the shop of a well-known dealer. 'A thousand francs' was the answer. 'And without the frame and signature?' The dealer, who was also a wit, replied, 'Oh, then you can have it for 3 francs 50.'

How often have we watched an art lover peering at a corner of a picture, anxiously searching for the signature that will tell them whether or not to be spellbound. For it should be mentioned that names may be used for black as well as white magic; in which former case they act as curses. When, for instance, a Rembrandt happens to bear the signature of one of his followers, let us say Ferdinand Bol, in the eyes of the world the picture loses the greater part of both its artistic and monetary value – something we shall be speaking of in a later chapter.

Writing of the well-known modern forgers Han van Meegeren (1889–1947), Elmyr de Hory (1911–76) and Tom Keating, Mark Jones says: 'Their fame rests more on the prestige of the artists whose work they imitated than any talent of their own. Name is indeed everything.'[28] In view of this situation the art forger should not disdain the assistance of a little sorcery, both to enhance his reputation and to send his works out into the world with the advantage of a good name. We must, however, be parsimonious in our use of the signatures as such, especially on early drawings. For it was not until the artist ceased to regard himself as an anonymous craftsman but rather as an individual possessed of a unique and inimitable talent that he thought of advertising himself with a signature. Had he reflected further on the matter he might have realized that if his work were really and truly inimitable it would not stand in need of a signature – it would sign itself.

But even with the advent of signatures on works of art, they were rarely employed on drawings. This was because by far the greater number of Old Master drawings were made in preparation for works of art completed in other media, such as painting, sculpture, stained glass, architecture, tapestry, etc. To regard these preliminary drawings as worthy of a signature would have seemed very curious indeed to artists who frequently destroyed their sketches, studies, cartoons and modelli as soon as they had served their constructional purpose. Consequently, before the eighteenth century, signed drawings are normally restricted to a few highly finished drawings, intended to function as independent works of art.

A notable exception to the rule are those signatures in the form of monograms that frequently occur on drawings of the German school. The practice would seem to have been introduced by such engravers as Albrecht Dürer, Martin Schongauer (*c*.1430–91) and Albrecht Altdorfer (*c*.1485–1538). These artists published and offered their prints for sale in editions, and they included their monogram to protect themselves from plagiarism, a practice they extended to their drawings. Incidentally, Dürer's plan to protect his copyright with his initials was not a conspicuous success. The great Italian engraver Marcantonio Raimondi (*c*.1480–*c*.1534) made copperplate engravings in imitation of the German's woodcuts of the *Life of the Virgin* (1510) and the *Small Passion* (1511), the former complete with Dürer's monogram. These he sold as originals through the Venetian publishers Niccolò and Domenico dal Gesù. Whether or not Raimondi did this with fraudulent intention has been much disputed. The fact that he signed one plate thus, exactly as Dürer himself had, tends to look bad:

ALBRECHT .

DUERER

NORICOS

FACIEBAT

1504

But, after all, the Italian was a reproductive engraver, and what kind of reproduction is it that misses out an important inscription? Anyway, Dürer himself was incensed at the idea of someone else profiting from his reputation, and we are told by Vasari that the artist complained to the Signoria di Venezia. Exactly what their ruling was is not clear. Although they seem to have prohibited Raimondi from using the Nuremberg master's monogram, the prints bearing the offending initials were certainly not called in for destruction as such prints occasionally turn up on the market even today. Having gained in respectability, they are eagerly sought by collectors happy to buy the work of two great engravers, Raimondi-Dürer, for the price of one.

At this point, like Raimondi, you may wish to attach a spellbinding name to your work, and you will be pleased to know that you may do so with a good conscience, for all you are doing in reality is making an inscription. Lawyers would not view the signing of your drawing 'Rembrandt', let us say, as forgery, because a drawing is not, legally speaking, a document.

When using such an important name as Rembrandt's the forger would have to be very naive to imagine that any expert is going to believe in it. At best they are going to think of it as an over-optimistic attribution, and if the drawing is sufficiently convincing as far as age is concerned and closely following the master's manner, it may be attributed to one of Rembrandt's many pupils: this is success.

But let us say that your drawing is not at all in the style of Rembrandt and yet nevertheless bears his illustrious name. Imagine for a moment that you have, in fact, drawn in the manner of van Dyck (1599–1641) and inscribed it 'Rembrandt'. This is diabolical. Are there no limits to your skulduggery? What you are doing will lead some poor unsuspecting authority in all innocence to deceive himself by reasoning along these lines: 'Here is an interesting old drawing wrongly ascribed to Rembrandt – who could the real draughtsman be?' Naturally the expert will not think of you or me straight away, and assuming you have been successful in giving your work the freshness and spontaneity of an authentic van Dyck the temptation will be very strong for him to continue his reasoning like this: 'How clever of me to have spotted a wrong attribution; more clever still if at the same time I have discovered an unrecorded van Dyck. Yes, yes, the more one looks at it the more like van Dyck it becomes; what an exciting discovery!'

I played this trick successfully with a drawing I once made in the manner of Parri Spinelli (1387–1453). I wrote the impossibly important name of Giotto on it and then put a line through it to suggest some former connoisseur had had doubts about such a grand attribution. This drawing was bought by one of the most important British art historians of his generation, Denys Sutton (d.1991).

To make a convincing copy of a signature requires much practice. I was taught a useful method by a gentleman sitting at a bar in Rome. His name was Booth, and he claimed to be a descendant of the man who shot Abraham Lincoln. When he told me this I was reminded of the lady who on being acquainted with Darwin's theory of evolution remarked: 'Well, if it's true that we are descended from apes, we should at least have the decency to keep quiet about it.' Anyway, having failed to convince the barman to accept a certain type of $50 bill as payment, Mr Booth turned to me and proposed to let me in on a priceless secret in exchange for a few drinks. He explained to me that in his profession he frequently found himself in the embarrassing position of holding traveller's cheques in need of a signature to make them negotiable. He had therefore been obliged to cultivate the art of penmanship in order to imitate any signature that might come his way. To prove his claim, he asked me to write my name on a blank sheet of paper. Then, hiding his work from me with his left hand, he made a copy of it; handing me back the paper, he asked, with a note of pride, 'Which one of these signatures is yours?' They were indistinguishable, and as one was directly above the other I could not begin to guess whether he had written my name above or below the original. Complimenting him on his skill, I agreed to pay his price for a lesson in penmanship and never was money better spent.

His method was simplicity itself. Having explained that one should ideally have the same kind of pen as the one with which the original was written, he went on to say that the penman should not view the signature he is copying as a series of letters but rather as an abstract line or series of lines. Reading the letters tends to distract one's attention from the abstract qualities of the line itself. To avoid this distraction and to concentrate on the movements that matter it is a great help to turn the signature upside down and make one's copy below it like this:

The rest is practice; eventually you will learn to copy a signature at the same speed as the original writer, thus producing the same natural flow of lines. Here follow some signatures for you to practise with. They have mostly been made with a dip pen, so to make your copies convincing you should also use the same type of pen. As you will probably have to practise each

Degas

Luellinus

B. Tiepolo 1750

P. Cezanne

TITIANV
S
EQVES
CES
F
1 5 4 3

Ant·van Dÿck·fecit

Ian. Van Huysum fecit

Bernard Bellotto dit Canaletto
Peintre Du Roi

Jacob Arigpmini La ican Pinx
1773

Dr Goúsv· Ferguson Æc.

Claude ~ Monet

N Poussin.

éd. Manet

BRVEGEL 1360

Marc Chagall

Jheronimus bosch

Rembrandt f. 164

signature several times, it might be a good idea to have a number of photo-copies made of pp. 65–7. I don't imagine you will ever have much use for van Eyck's signature, but it is a splendid piece of calligraphy and should prove a challenging exercise.

Monograms

In my youth I lodged with an elderly couple called Mr and Mrs Gibbs. It was Mr Gibbs who taught me something, if not exactly about monograms, at least about initials in general. He was a kindly old fellow, and knowing that I was hard up he would save his used razor-blades for subsequent employment on the fluff that was then appearing on my chin. He showed me how to resharpen these flexible blades by rubbing them round and round on the inside of a damp glass. On one occasion when I was away from home for a few weeks he sent me a small package containing razor-blades and a covering note. The note was signed Albert Gibbs RA. On my return I questioned him about the initials after his name, saying that I had no idea he was an artist, and a Royal Academician at that! 'No, no,' he demurred. 'RA stands for Royal Artillery.' Apparently he had served with the Royal Artillery during the First World War.

Similarly, Albrecht Dürer's renowned monogram, AD, together with the date, was intended as a pun on Anno Domini. The various possible interpretations of any given set of initials has from time to time caused real embarrassment to experts, and not only in the field of art. For example, after a lengthy study of what he believed to be an ancient pot inscribed MJDD, a member of the French Academy of Inscriptions was able to decipher the initials as an abbreviation of the phrase: *Magno Jovi Deorum Deo* ('To the Great Jupiter, God of Gods'). This scholar was somewhat discomfited to learn later that the pot was not an antiquity at all but a modern mustard jar, and the letters stood for *Moutarde Jaune de Dijon* (Yellow Dijon Mustard).

All this means that you may use initials, and monograms incorporating initials, as freely as you please, and let the experts decide what you mean by them. In this way you may put Dürer's initials on a drawing and mean any number of things by it other than the great artist's name or Anno Domini. Anything from 'After Dürer' to 'After Dinner': just keep your little joke to yourself, and let others think what they will. Opposite are some examples of monograms and initials you might one day find useful. Try copying them for practice.

Inscriptions

Inscriptions on drawings are made by various people for various reasons. On his drawing the artist himself may write the subject-matter, the time and place where it was made or make colour notes, etc. Sometimes the artist's inscription is unrelated to the drawing, being anything from a shopping list to the draft of a letter. Collectors may also have written their comments and observations, usually on the backs of drawings. Dealers may have put prices (sometimes in code), catalogue numbers, stock numbers and so on. Owners may have written on drawings the names of the sitters or some family tradition; framemakers, details concerning the colour of the mount, the measurement of the margins or the type of moulding for the frame. Numbers are also frequently found on old drawings.

To make a convincing inscription one must do quite a lot of research, otherwise it is very easy to make mistakes of one kind or another. The general rule is only to make inscriptions when it would seem odd that there was none. For example, Edward Lear (1812–88), the English topographical draughtsman and the celebrated author of *A Book of Nonsense* (1846), virtually always wrote on his drawings made on the spot: the place, the date, the time of day, the direction of the wind, the local colours and so on. To come across one of his drawings done from nature and lacking such annotations would, though not damning, be curious. Similarly, the Dutch painter and etcher Roelandt Savery (*c.*1576–1639), whose drawings of peasants so long passed as works by Jan Breughel the Elder (1568–1625), also made copious marks on his drawings; to find an unrecorded drawing from the series with perfectly convincing writing on it to match the known sheets would speak very strongly of the work's authenticity. On the other hand, if the inscriptions were in the slightest way suspect the drawing would be dismissed. Remember, the magic of words is, of all spells, the most dangerous. All things considered, I would suggest that the use of false inscriptions, if indulged in at all, should be kept to the absolute minimum. After all, a good drawing needs no boost from an inscription, and a bad one remains bad whatever is written on it.

Collectors' Marks

Collectors of the past frequently stamped their drawings with a distinguishing mark. The better ones showed respect for their possessions by making these marks small and placing them discreetly in a corner or on the

negl'ornak
e nell Universalità
di tutto il genere d' Pittura
bellezza buontà vaghezza e
loggiadria Perino passò tutti i
moderni, e gl'Antichi. fu alle
uato da una Capra, hebbe da sette
maestri poi al Carbone e M.A. e sotto Raff

·DESEGNI·DE·VARIE·P
·RACOLTI·PER·ANT·
·II·PICTORE·D·LANN
GNORE·M·CCCCC·

Disegno Capitalissimo
di
Perino dal Vago;
era nella Collezione di
Giorgio Vasari.

Mr Gütier has seen the Original of this with

Your Friend but gives the Bag you had before
Friendship would fain, but Friendship Canno more

Mr Richardson Sen.r was fond of this Design, & always called it one of his me
to explain his meaning, he would Lecture away, &say. here is no Art to ketch the
of Opposition between light & shadow, which is not the true Idea of the Cloro-scure
& dabbs of Shadow to each other, but by regular gradations, falling easily & natura
& Guercino, may have succeeded thro' superior Skill, yet most of their Apish Imita
=tempts to doe the same, here is no tedious delicacy, in an Affectation of high finis
& time thrown away upon a Drawing, no such laboured Slavish Correctness, as ,

acheté ce qu'equil qui l'avois apprie en Hollande
dans un des p.r voyages qu'il y fit. J'nen ai pen
vu a mieux conditionnés. Les planches ne regarn
repuis quelques années, mais il s'en faut beaucoup
qu'elles donnent d'aussi bonnes epreuves que le
feu ces premiers / ci /

Ab hæredibus Jac. Stella Pictoris Regii olim accipiebat à Pet. Crozat.

se non di m.o sua di mano d'Orazio suo figlio

P Resta

back or on the mount. Others proclaimed their ownership in no uncertain terms with huge marks, which sometimes disfigure the prints and drawings to which they are appended. Sometimes these collectors' marks are highly decorative, but whether attractive or otherwise they speak of the drawing's history and are of considerable interest to the connoisseur. Should the mark be that of a highly respected authority such as eighteenth-century French collector P.-J. Mariette, then any attribution he may have attached to the drawing, or any account of its provenance, will be given very serious consideration.

As a beginner I made some very clumsy attempts at faking collectors' marks. I had two principal methods, both of which, with more experience than I then possessed, can in fact produce perfectly acceptable results. The first method was to have a line block, or zincs, made by a printer and then to ink it with printer's ink and lay the drawing face down upon it. Next, making sure the paper does not move, burnish the area with one's fingernail or the back of a teaspoon. The second method is to take a sufficiently transparent sheet of paper (not tracing-paper) and carefully trace the design on to it with dark pencil lines that will show through to the other side. Now, taking the pencil lines as a guide, redraw the mark in reverse on the back in watercolour. This done, and the watercolour dry, dampen the area of the drawing that is to receive the mark. Laying your watercolour copy face downward on to the drawing, rub with your nail or spoon as for printing from a line block. It is advisable with both methods to print the mark once or twice beforehand so that the impression on the drawing is not too black and fresh looking.

Better and simpler than these methods is to have a photocopy made of the design from Fritz Lugt's *Les Marques de collections de dessins et d'estampes*, published in Amsterdam in 1921 and reprinted with a supplement in 1956 (one of the musts for the forger's bookshelf), and take it to a professional sealcutter. If you are a skilled engraver, you can engrave the marks yourself on boxwood. This is a method I have used on occasion, but it is tedious, and as one should, for obvious reasons, avoid using the same mark more than once or twice '*il gioco non vale la candela*' (the game is not worth the candle).

The design of collectors' marks can be very decorative, and as the majority of them are well over 50 years old they may be used without infringing the copyright law. Furthermore, if they incorporate the initials of the collector they are, in fact, monograms and open to the same interpretations.

Nevertheless, I would advise you to use them sparingly for the same reasons as one should be parsimonious with signatures, monograms and inscriptions. Good drawings speak for themselves, and a faked provenance, if discovered, will call them into doubt; bad drawings are not worth the trouble involved. If you should use collectors' marks, make sure you do your homework. That is, at least make sure that the collector was not dead when the artist he was supposed to be collecting was not yet born.

P. J. Mariette
(1694–1774), Paris
Drawings and prints

Count of Bardi,
Italy

Milford.

Baron Milford (1744–1823),
Picton Castle, Haverfordwest
(Pembrokeshire) – Old Master drawings

R. Cosway (1740–1820),
London – Drawings & prints

Earl Spencer.
Althorp
Old Master drawings

J. Beitscher
(20th century),
Berlin,
Old Master drawings

Count (?) Gelozzi
or Gelosi
Drawings

A. P. Leroux (1870–1950),
France – Old Master drawings

P. J. Mariette
(1694–1774),
Paris,
Drawings and prints

PART TWO

Old Master Paintings

Dates for the Introduction of Painting Materials

Prehistory *Chalk and other natural earths*

Charcoal black

Lamp black

Red and yellow ochre

Haematite (an iron ore of deep red)

Antiquity *Azurite* (a blue copper ore)

Malachite (a green copper ore)

Cinnabar (a red produced from a natural compound of mercury and sulphur)

Orpiment (a natural compound of arsenic and sulphur producing a golden yellow)

8th century *Vermilion* (probably in use much earlier)

10th century Recipes for *boiled oil* and *stand oil* given by Heraclius

13th century Genuine *ultramarine* (produced from lapis lazuli)

Early 15th century Oil painting begins to establish itself

*c.*1470 *Azurite* (of exceptional quality)

16th century *Blue* and *green bice* (artificial copper ores)

Smalt (cobalt glass)

*c.*1590 *Turpentine*

*c.*1660 Latest date for *azurite*

18th century *Prussian blue* (discovered in 1704 but first used in painting *c.*1776)

Late 18th century Invention of the power loom, which gradually led to hand-woven canvas being replaced with the machine product c.1750–1850 *Bitumen* (asphaltum: an unstable pigment mostly employed between these dates)

1797 *Chrome yellow* (not used in painting until somewhat later)

1802 *Cobalt blue* (not used in painting until somewhat later)

1828 *Artificial ultramarine* (not used in painting until somewhat later)

1840 *Zinc white*

1851 *Cadmium yellow*

1862 *Chromes* (yellow, orange, red and green)

1930 *Titanium white*

CHAPTER SEVEN

Grounds for Action

*'You please me much by saying that no other fault is to be found in
your picture than the roughness of the surface; for that part being
of use in giving effect at a proper distance and what a judge of
painting knows an original from a copy by.'*

THOMAS GAINSBOROUGH TO A CLIENT

We live in an age of fabulous fakes. For instance, photography combined with the most sophisticated of printing techniques has made it possible to reproduce prints and drawings in facsimiles that are virtually indistinguishable from the originals. This situation has given rise to the forgery of artists' prints to an extent that has truly been termed industrial. Salvador Dalí (1904–89), that arch-forger of his own work, seems to have founded the industry by signing 20,000 blank sheets of paper for lithographs he had never seen. But as Paul Webster and Ian Kanz point out: 'The flood of Dalís might pale in relation to a spectacular American case, in which a septuagenarian grandmother and her two daughters turned out fake Dalí, Picasso, Chagall, Matisse and Miró prints with conveyor-belt efficiency. The reassuringly named Centre Art Galleries raked in an estimated $2.6 billion from such forgeries.'

Since then, the New York-based International Forum for Arts Research has refused to authenticate prints by a number of modern painters. According to Nancy Little, who works on the Authentication Service, so many prints were spurious, or questionable, that they could not handle any more. 'We couldn't get any other work done,' she said.

The point I would like to make here is that artists' prints, apart from a plate-mark and a slightly embossed line in original etchings, are flat, and our modern reproductive techniques are able to make a convincing approximation of their generally smooth, two-dimensional images. When, however, it comes to reproducing paintings, none of the present reproductive techniques is able to give us the tactile values of an original: neither the thickness of the impasto, nor the thin transparencies of the glazes, nor the broken texture of the scumbled areas. The result is that nobody with any experience of real paintings would be deceived for a moment by a photographic reproduction of one, because the three-dimensional quality of the original would be lacking.

As it happens, there are a number of very skilful copyists of Old Master paintings. As they are using paint, brush and canvas, just as the original artists did, one might imagine that they would perhaps succeed where mechanical means have so far failed and successfully imitate the qualities so conspicuously absent from the machine-made article. But this is not so, the reason being that they are working very much as the camera works. That is to say they are looking only at the surface of the picture and do not, as a rule, know by what process this surface was created. Usually they attempt to reproduce with one layer of paint a surface that was, in fact, the result of many layers. In addition to this (which, in itself, gives a very flat effect) they often use a ready-prepared canvas, whose mechanical grain shows through their meagre paint surface in such a way as to give the impression of a photographic reproduction printed on canvas. No matter how accurate they may be in their outlines and colouring (usually copied from a photograph or on a photographic base) no knowledgeable person would be convinced that their pictures were anything more than clever but lifeless copies.

What the good forger knows is what the good gardener knows: the answer lies in the ground. The final layer of paint or varnish depends for its effect on everything that underlies and supports it. The panel or canvas, the glue, the ground or priming, the underpainting, the upperpainting, the glazes and varnishes all interact to create a whole of a richness and beauty that no single layer of paint or printer's ink can come anywhere near to imitating. With the rapid advances in technology this may, of course, not be true tomorrow, but meanwhile we have to get to understand the actual materials and methods of the masters themselves.

Panel

In the seventeenth century the Dutch government passed a law forbidding the manufacture of panels unless produced on behalf of the government itself. The reason for this monopoly was stated in these terms.

> The genius of an artist is the patrimony of his country, and the former has the duty of guaranteeing the longest possible duration to the masterpieces to which he may give birth. That this may be assured, equal precautions must be taken in regard to all paintings, as it be understood that a painter, however celebrated he may become, always begins by being unknown. Furthermore, he may happen by chance to be modest and in consequence ignorant of the later value of any work he may be undertaking and so must not be allowed to compromise its existence by negligence or economy.[29]

From this it is clear that not the first piece of wood, or the first carpenter upon whom one might have happened, was considered suitable for the production of a good panel, and a look at the back of some of the panel pictures from the period shows the justice of this view. Some of the panels are themselves works of art, having an elaborate, flexible kind of cradling (an interlocking series of supports to prevent, or counteract, warping brought on by changes of temperature), the work of highly skilled joiners or cabinet-makers. Sometimes the cradling was added later to correct a panel that had already warped, and this brings us to one of the big problems with panel pictures: their tendency to bend out of shape or split due to changes in humidity.

The best precaution against warping and cracking is to use thoroughly seasoned wood, and no wood could be more seasoned than that of a truly old panel picture. Artistically worthless old pictures on wood do come up for sale from time to time, and these provide the support that suits our purpose best. Panels from old furniture are also desirable. Unfortunately they are no less desirable to our colleagues engaged in the making of new 'antique' furniture, so we may have to pay quite a lot for them. If you are obliged to use fresh timber for decorative work it must be seasoned. Cennino Cennini recommends boiling the panel in water, and this corresponds to a modern method of hastening the seasoning process by steaming. The best method, however, is slow air drying. The panels are cut in the summer and stored where air may circulate about them until the following summer, when it will be found that some have warped or cracked but those that have not will be safe to work on.

Preparation of a ground for panel painting in tempera

Having obtained a suitable panel we must now turn our attention to preparing it for painting upon. Our principal source of information concerning the preparation of panels during Italy's finest period of tempera painting is Cennino Cennini's celebrated *Il libro dell'arte,* to which, as it is easily obtainable in a modern edition, I refer the reader for more detailed instructions. What follows here is an outline of Cennini's method with some comments that may throw further light upon it.

In the first place it must be remembered that Cennini is speaking of panels prepared for painting in 'tempera'; that is to say the medium, or vehicle, with which the pigments are to be mixed is egg in one form or another. We shall be speaking of the egg-tempera technique below. Because of the widespread use of eggs as a binder, the word tempera has come to be used exclusively for painting in which egg is used as the medium, but the early Italian writers used the term tempera for colours mixed or 'tempered' with other vehicles as well, such as glue or oil.

In chapter CXIII of his book Cennini tells us 'How to begin to paint pictures'. After recommending poplar-, lime- and willow-wood he says that the panel must be made 'quite smooth'. What he intends by this becomes clear when he tells us to remove any defects such as knots and nails, but he is careful to add: 'The surface of the panel must not be too smooth.' The reason for this is that we are going to lay a ground of gesso on to the panel, and naturally the important thing is to remove the possibility of the gesso detaching itself. This is done by roughening the surface of the wood, not polishing it as some followers of Cennini have understood by his making the surface 'quite smooth'. The principle is exactly the same as that employed by the plasterer who scores lines into his first coat of coarse lime with his trowel to give a tooth to which his fine finishing coat will firmly adhere.

After this preliminary preparation the panel is sized much in the same way and for much the same purpose as we sized our old paper in the second chapter of this book. This is carried out with two coats of glue, the first one weaker than the second and the first coat allowed to dry before applying the second. It is here that Cennini tells us about 'the effect of the first glue. How a weak water, or liquor, is absorbed from it by the wood, which prepares the timber for the glue and grounds to be applied afterwards.' And he draws a parallel with a hungry man whose aperitif gives him an appetite for dinner.

In the following chapter of Cennini's book he speaks of 'how to fasten linen on panels'. This must be 'old, fine and white' and is attached with your 'best glue' and ideally on a dry and windy day in winter for 'glue is stronger in winter'. This attaching of linen or fine canvas on to a panel obviously will not only hold the panel together but also give a tooth, or texture, that will be helpful in gripping the gesso to be applied. Judging, however, from the surviving paintings from Cennini's day it was by no means the invariable practice, and gesso was frequently applied directly over the size.

Cennini's advice for laying a gesso ground is spread over five chapters. The process, as one may conveniently carry it out today, is essentially as follows.

1 APPLYING THE COARSE PLASTER

Take some ordinary plaster of the kind used by builders, which has the texture of flour (this is that which Cennini calls *gesso grosso* – coarse plaster). Put a small quantity at a time on to the slab that you will be using for mixing your paints. In Cennini's day this slab was of porphyry, but today you will find a thick sheet of plate-glass easier to acquire and just as service-able. Now you take a spatula and mix your plaster very thoroughly with size, just as if you were mixing or grinding a pigment with oil. You then apply this coarse plaster mixture generously to the panel with the spatula. This is left to dry for two or three days, at which point the surface is slightly roughened with a rasp or coarse sandpaper to give a grip to the fine plaster used in the finishing coats.

2 APPLYING FINE PLASTER

Cennini tells us that the painters of his time bought their fine plaster (*gesso soffile*) from the apothecaries, and similarly we may buy our fine plaster from a well-stocked modern chemist's shop. Under the name of dental plaster it is, or was, used by dentists for making casts of teeth. This fine plaster, which is as soft as silk between the fingers, is the same material as the coarse plaster mentioned above, but it has been treated by being well washed (slaked), a process that Cennini tells us takes at least a month. As with the coarse plaster, the fine variety is thoroughly mixed with size on the grinding-stone, or slab of glass, using a spatula. It is, however, applied to the panel not with the spatula but with a soft brush. The plaster is slightly heated to help the glue in it flow more easily, and the plaster mix must be of a stiff, creamy texture. Cennini recommends eight coats, the first of which should be rubbed with the fingers, the better to unite with the coarser plaster below. The coats are applied by changing the direction of the brushstrokes each time, that is alternating horizontal strokes with vertical ones. A little time is allowed to elapse between each coat but not long enough for the lower coat to dry right through.

Again the ground is left to dry in the shade for at least 48 hours, after which it may be smoothed with fine pumice (Cennini used charcoal dust) and then burnished with the kind of polishing tool used by etchers. We are told that the result will be 'as white as milk', and the importance of this being so will become apparent when we come to discuss the effect that the ground has on the subsequent layers of paint.

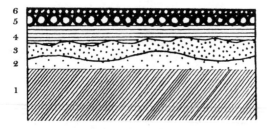

6. Gesso sottile (fine plaster)
5. Gesso grosso (coarse plaster)
4. Linen
3. Strong glue ⎫ Size
2. Weak glue ⎭
1. Panel

Diagram showing the various strata of Cennini's ground

Preparation of a panel for painting in oil
As has been suggested, Cennini's ground is ideally suited to tempera painting. Some artists have used it for oil painting, but this is only successful when the oil film is separated from the gesso ground by some isolating layer. This is because unless the ground contains an excessive amount of glue it readily absorbs the oil from the paints, something that is undesirable for both the ground and the paints. The ground becomes saturated with oil and turns yellow, thus no longer reflecting light through to the surface, and the colours lose all their lustre, becoming dull and lifeless. The two methods for isolating the ground most used are:

1. Put a coat of glue or shellac over the ground. (Vasari recommends 'four or five coats of the smoothest size' applied with a sponge.)[30]
2. Make an underpainting in tempera.

Neither of these two methods is ideal. The danger of putting glue or size over the plaster is that if it is strong enough to function it might in time flake off, taking the paint with it. Making the underpainting in tempera is technically sound if carried out with great care. The necessary thing to do is to ensure that in both the tempera and the oil layer the medium employed is mixed equally with the pigments throughout, otherwise the result will be patchy.

On the whole the safest method is to size the panel as for tempera, attach canvas or linen, if liked, and prime with an oil ground, as for priming canvas (*see* below). This was the method of Rubens and many Flemish and Dutch artists of the seventeenth century.

Naturally, if you have managed to procure a genuinely old panel with some miserable daub on it you will remove the daub leaving an authentic period ground. This ground will be covered with the most delightful cracks, which you will doubtless want to preserve right up to your final layer of paint. How to achieve this will be discussed below when dealing with 'ageing' techniques. Here we will continue with our discussion of supports and grounds.

Canvas

Vasari tells us that: 'In order to convey pictures from one place to another men have invented the convenient method of painting on canvas, which is of little weight and when rolled up is of easy transport.'[31] Perhaps because of this statement the use of canvas as a support has come to be thought of as an Italian Renaissance invention. Certainly its common use, if we are to believe Vasari, began in Venice, where as early as 1476 or thereabouts, Gentile Bellini (1429–1507) executed large pictures on canvas for the Hall of the Grand Council in the Ducal Palace. But, in fact, canvas was used as a support in ancient Egypt. Painting on canvas in ancient Rome is mentioned by Pliny in his *Historia Naturalis* (XXXV, 51), and the Netherlandish masters of the fifteenth century very rarely but sometimes used it. An example are the paintings for the Town Hall of Brussels by Rogier van der Weyden (*c*.1400–64).

The only canvas worthy of serious consideration is linen canvas. Cotton and hemp are just cheaper substitutes, but the worst is a mixture of cotton and linen because the tensile strength of the two materials is different. The linen canvas should be as thick and heavy as is compatible with the style of the master to be followed. A rule of thumb is the smaller the picture the finer should be the texture of the canvas. Very often, however, the forger has no choice in the matter and must use whatever old canvas he has been lucky enough to find; it will be a case of the canvas choosing the artist rather than vice versa.

There has been quite a lot written about the disadvantages of canvas as a support. Its greatest defect in the eyes of its detractors is its habit of reacting to any changes in humidity by contracting or expanding to a degree that prompted one authority to remark: 'It contracts and expands to such an extent as practically to guarantee cracking of the paint in the long run.' If the natural expansion and contraction of canvas might crack the paint a little sooner, it would save us quite a lot of trouble. As it is, we forgers have to exercise considerable ingenuity to get it to do sooner what it practically guarantees to do in the course of time.

Other defects of canvas – always according to those who do not know how to turn them to advantage – are:

1. It does not protect the painting from behind, leaving it vulnerable to attack from oxidation, damp and harmful fumes by penetration from the back.
2. The fibres become rotten or brittle, and eventually the picture has to be relined. There is scarcely any picture of value over 200 years old that has not been transferred to a new canvas.
3. It is fragile and easily ripped or punctured.

In short, canvas readily responds to any treatment we might feel a need to give it to imitate the signs of age. Here the same advice holds good as that given for the treatment of paper: if the canvas is truly old it needs no ageing. And, again as for paper, any unsightly damage should be neatly repaired – more of which later. Now, having introduced the subject of painting on canvas, we must speak of how our canvas is stretched upon a frame of wood and then of the kind of grounds, or priming, that are suitable for use upon it.

How to stretch canvas

If you have found an old canvas it is most likely to be already stretched upon the wooden framework that we call a stretcher. If the stretcher is an old one, it is a valuable aid to creating an aura of authenticity about your 'Old' Master. If it is not old, it will in no way affect an expert's judgement as to the age of the painting on it, for he knows as well as we do that old paintings are frequently relined and put on sound, modern stretchers. In any case the faker of Old Master paintings will often have occasion to stretch or restretch a canvas, and this is how one proceeds.

The tools necessary are a canvas stretcher and a small hammer for knocking in tacks. The canvas stretcher is a specially designed pincer-type tool that grips the edge of the canvas between two flat bars of metal and allows one to strain the canvas by leverage. This can be bought in most art-supply stores. If you are restretching the canvas you will have carefully preserved the old rusty tacks with which it was previously attached. These you will be putting into different holes to show that the painting has, in fact, been restretched. You have nothing to gain by hiding the truth here. But if, on the other hand, the canvas has been cut down, you may be using new tacks, and these are best left for a few weeks in a little water to rust a bit before use. You will also remember to stretch this newly stretched canvas twice to give the appearance that it was formerly on another stretcher. This is crucial if your stretcher is modern. Here is how to stretch your canvas.

1. Lay your canvas face downward on a flat surface, setting aside the stretcher pegs – these are the little wedges at the corners that are knocked in to stretch the canvas and loosened to allow the canvas to slacken.

2. Make sure the corners of your stretcher are true by testing the inside of them for a 90° angle with a set square.

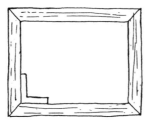

3. Place the stretcher on to the canvas, which must, of course, be slightly larger to allow for turning over the sides. The sides of the stretcher must be parallel with the weave of the canvas. At this stage the dust of centuries, taken from the vacuum cleaner, may be introduced between the frame and the canvas.

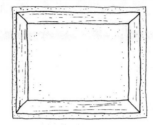

4. Knock in one of the large-head tacks in the middle of one side of the stretcher. Strain the canvas away from this tack and drive in another tack directly opposite it. Repeat this with the other sides so that you have four tacks in the position as shown in the following diagram.

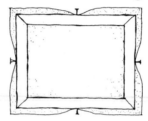

5. Two other tacks are now placed to the right and left, respectively, of the first four, stretching the canvas as necessary each time.

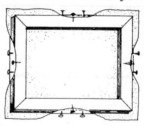

6. Continue to drive in the tacks two by two, always stretching the canvas in the same manner until the corners are reached, when the canvas should be folded like this:

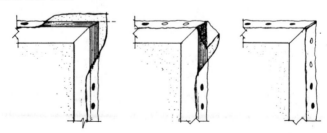

The corners are best stretched with the fingers rather than the canvas stretcher. This leaves a little play for the wedges or keys which are now delicately tapped in, a little at a time, so that they are all in place more or less at the same moment.

Preparation of the ground

The essential difference between a ground that is suitable for priming a canvas as opposed to a panel is that it must have a certain amount of flexibility. Obviously the gesso ground described above would not lend itself to being rolled up or follow the shrinkage and expansion of the linen fibres. For this reason the grounds used on canvas are generally made from a combination of white pigment and oil.

SIZING CANVAS

But before applying these grounds the canvas must be sized, just as the panels and papers are sized. Unless you deliberately want to make your ground to crack or fall off, the glue should not be too strong. Test it with your fingers. It should be strong enough to stick your thumb and forefinger together but not so strong that you have to use any force to separate them. To see if your canvas has been correctly sized, wait until it is dry and hold it at an angle to the light and see to what extent it shines. If the whole surface has a smooth gloss, then the glue is far too strong; if the surface is totally matt then the size is far too weak; but if the glue glistens in the interstices of the canvas, like stars seen through a mist, then it is just right. Only one coat of size is necessary for canvas.

GLUE GROUNDS

Glue grounds are essentially made of three ingredients: whiting, glue and something to add elasticity. This third ingredient in the old recipes is nearly always edible; honey, glycerine, milk or cheese being common ones. Here is a basic recipe:

125g (4oz) whiting (as used for making whitewash, or *calce* in Italian)
1 level teaspoon of powdered glue

Heat the ingredients together in a double boiler, together with sufficient milk to form a thin cream. The mixture should be thoroughly stirred until the glue is melted down and applied warm. This ground is good for tempera painting, but, as with all gesso or whiting grounds, it is too absorbent for use with oils.

This recipe may be varied in any number of ways: gesso may be used in place of whiting; the type and quantity of glue may be varied; or a little glycerine added. Indeed, the possibilities for experiment are virtually endless.

Lying between glue grounds and oil grounds are those that contain, in addition to the ingredients that give the pigment, the binder and the elastifier. All of these may be varied, providing what is used possesses the necessary quality. There are even recipes containing a little oil, and the following pâte is taken from A. Desaint's *Trucs d'Atelier* (Paris, 1913).[32]

PÂTE ANGLAISE
For one kilogram (2lb)
500g (1lb) whiting
250g (8oz) glue
175g (6oz) resin
60g (2oz) linseed oil
Mix well together, melting the resin in the oil. May be kept for a few days by wrapping in a damp cloth.

All glue grounds can be made less absorbent in a similar way to that mentioned above. For rendering Cennino Cennini's gesso ground less absorbent it may be:

1. Given a coat of size.
2. Sprayed with a retouching varnish.
3. Coated with flake white (white lead) tempered with yolk of egg.

But all this seems to me to be making the best of a bad job. If one wants a non-absorbent ground for oil painting, do as the Old Masters did and make it non-absorbent right from the start by using a ground in which the binding medium is oil.

OIL GROUNDS
The basic recipe for the oil grounds of the Old Masters is simply flake white mixed with oil. To this some authorities advise adding a little whiting and/ or resin. But there seems to be no real advantage in complicating matters. Certainly flake white ground in oil without further additions seems to have been good enough for most of the Old Masters painting in oils. Nowadays there is a great outcry against the use of flake white because, as white lead, it is supposed to be poisonous. Doubtless it is, but the painters of the past seem to have thrived on it. Titian (*c.*1487–1576) used it for the whole of his

long working life and died at around the age of 90, not of lead poisoning but the plague (an old teacher of mine used to say that if the plague had not taken the master away, he would be still with us). Tubes of flake white often have a health warning on them, and it has long been illegal in France to sell it in powder form. But dangerous or otherwise it is an essential pigment for the forger; the other whites available, zinc and titanium, were not known to the Old Masters, and it is quite impossible to simulate some of the qualities of the crisp brushwork found in old painting with these more modern colours, which tend to be slimy.

Some flake white on the market is really a mixture of lead white and zinc white. To test these whites a little of the pigment is taken up on a spatula and gently roasted over an alcohol flame; the lead white should turn permanently yellow, the zinc white temporarily so. One of the drawbacks of flake white for the ground is that it is a relatively slow dryer. To remedy this, some of the Old Masters ground it together with a little pigment of a quick-drying, or siccative, nature, such as raw or burnt umber, but this takes away a little of the whiteness from the ground, which, as we shall see below, is not desirable. Sir Arthur Church, in *The Chemistry of Paints and Painting* (London, 1901), recommends the addition of borate or oxalate of manganese as a dryer, but in my experience time and patience are the best siccatives.

The main reason why an oil priming must be thoroughly dry is that when linseed oil (the oil mostly used) is quite hardened it is much less absorbent than at the beginning of the drying process and consequently does not suck the oil from the paint laid upon it. In other words it is the hardened oil that gives to our ground the non-absorbent quality that we are looking for in our oil priming.

When laying the ground, it is as well to put on at least three coats, as the Old Masters were not as skimpy with their grounds as today's suppliers of artists' materials, whose products normally suffer from their desire to save on costs. Before painting on an oil ground it should be lightly sandpapered to give a bite for the subsequent layers of paint.

Old Grounds

The above grounds are, of course, only employed in the absence of a genuinely old ground, revealed by cleaning off an old painting from a panel or canvas. The methods of removing the old paint vary according to the type of picture in hand. Normally a solvent is used. Alcohol and acetone are the two most generally employed, and these act on a wide range of paints and varnishes. The solvent is mixed with a restrainer (turpentine or rectified petroleum) so that we can control its action. Tests are made on the painting to ensure that we are in control of the situation and that the solvent will remove the old paint only down to the ground. In stripping off a picture the restrainer must constantly be at hand, and the operator holds two swabs of cotton-wool, one impregnated with the solvent mixture and the other with the restrainer. At the very first sign of any softening of the ground, such as a trace of its whiteness on the stripping swab, the area is at once flooded with the restrainer to arrest the action of the solvent. The swab used for removing the paint and varnish should frequently be changed so that one can clearly follow one's progress.

Friction is another way of removing paint and varnish. There are small mechanical sanders, using sandpaper available from almost any hardware store, and these are very efficient.

A third method is to use a commercial paint stripper. In this case a small area of the picture is tested to determine how much time is required for the corrosive substance to eat its way down to the ground. When this is established it is a straightforward procedure to coat the picture with the paint stripper and, watch in hand, remove the unwanted paint with a spatula before any damage is done to the ground. If you should strip off a painting it must be done very thoroughly otherwise the X-ray machine may be your undoing.

Bleaching an old ground

You may find that your old ground has greatly yellowed, and it is of the utmost importance that it should be as white as possible (a point to be explained below). You may bleach the ground by applying to it a sheet or sheets of blotting-paper that have been soaked in hydrogen peroxide or some other bleaching agent. Should this for some reason fail to work, then you must lay a new ground on top of the old one in such a way as not to fill up the old cracks.

How to lay a new ground over an old one

Take some white lead in powder form and make it into a stiffish paste with linseed oil. When well mixed, put a little on to a sheet of plate-glass. Then, with a hard rubber roller, such as is used for printing linocuts and wood-engraving, roll out the paint exactly as though it were printing ink. You now roll the paint thinly over the old ground in such a way as it does not fill the old cracks. To do this the paint must not be in the least bit runny, and a good plan is to remove any excess oil by rolling the paint out a second time on newspaper before rolling it over the old ground. To facilitate seeing whether or not the cracks are being filled, they may be stained with diluted ink.

The importance of a white ground

On one of my first visits to a picture gallery I was admiring a fine marine painting by J. M. W. Turner (1775–1851). The sea was fearfully rough, and one could almost hear the crash of the waves as they thundered towards the bottom edge of the frame. There were some wretched shipwrecked sailors clinging to a fragile raft that was about to be torn apart by the mountainous waves. As I was imagining their fate, from a proper distance to see the picture as a whole, I felt a sudden impulse to step further backward, which I did. On reflection, I realized that Turner's picture had worked on my subconscious, and I had instinctively acted as I would have done had real waves been threatening to burst the frame and overwhelm me, that is to say to get out of danger. This experience reminded me of a contemporary cartoon showing Turner retouching one of his paintings on Varnishing Day at the Royal Academy. The great artist is shown standing on a stepladder, palette and brush in hand, working on a brilliant sunset, which casts a shadow of the painter on the gallery floor. The cartoonist's amusing comment has, in fact, a certain amount of basis of truth. Turner's magical pictures are lit up and gain their life from within. For like other great painters of the past he knew the value of a pure white ground and how to exploit it to the full.

As we all know, Turner was not only a painter in oils but also a water-colourist, and some would have him be the greatest of painters in that medium. Now the secret of the artist's success in oils stems from his transfer-ring his knowledge of watercolour to the oil medium. The basic principle of watercolour is the use of transparent washes of colour on white paper, the paper providing the white where required and shining through everywhere. A good watercolour depends on the same optical principle as gives brilliance to the work of the so-called Italian primitives working with thin colour on Cennino Cennini's pure white gesso ground.

Between the sound craftsmanlike painting of the fourteenth and fifteenth centuries, and Turner's partial return to their technique in the 1800s, painters' methods were constantly changing. New aesthetic aims demanded new techniques (a process that, of course, is still going on), but one thing remained constant among the finest painters, and that is the use of a white ground. Titian, Rembrandt, Rubens and Velasquez (1599–1660) to mention just a few (the list would be endless), all used a white priming. To understand why one has only to make a little experiment. Take a small, unprimed board or canvas; prime half of it white and the other half with any colour that contains no white. When thoroughly dry, paint anything you please on it, allowing the colours to cross over from one side to the other. Vary the thickness of your paint from thin glazes to thick impasto with semi-solid painting in between. You will not have to work long before you realize that the colours on the non-white side will have no life in them except perhaps the thickly painted lighter areas. It is true that the Old Masters frequently tinted their grounds with a light grey or brown, but they took great care to keep this tint translucent so that the pure white ground would still give life to the colours above.

There is another good reason why the Old Masters should have used a white ground, and this has to do with the nature of linseed oil. This oil darkens with age while at the same time becoming more translucent. Consequently its increase in darkness is to some extent compensated for by more light passing through it from the ground, and a certain balance is maintained, preventing the picture from becoming too gloomy. Incidentally, the property of oil to become more translucent with age has led some chemists to imagine that by measuring the refraction of light through any given sample of oil and thereby determining its 'refractive index' they can determine the age of it. The analytic chemist A. P. Laurie, Professor of Chemistry at the Royal Academy of Arts, London, was the first champion of this method of detecting fakes in the first decade of this century. It is one of those ever-so-comforting theories trotted out by science from time to time to keep the nervous collector happy. Unfortunately, or fortunately for us, it doesn't work. The first difficulty for the chemist is isolating a sufficiently large particle of old oil that has not been stained. The real obstacle, however, is the insurmountable one of not knowing what the oil's refractive index was when the picture was painted. There is no fixed amount of translucency for all freshly produced oils, nor is it known whether all oils, even when of the same kind, increase in transparency at the same rate, or to what extent individual environments affect the process. Without this information the scientific investigator can come to no certain conclusion. All of which means we may carry on as before.

CHAPTER EIGHT

War Paint

'I give you this advice, that you endeavour always to use fine gold and good colours, particularly in painting representations of our Lady... And even if you are not well paid, God and our Lady will reward your soul and body for it.'

CENNINO CENNINI

Your ground laid, or better still uncovered, you will now be keen to prepare your paints, consider your medium and your oils and varnishes, select your brushes, all according to the methods employed by the Old Masters you aim to follow. So let us first examine the pigments, the powdered colours that we are to mix with a binding medium to produce our paints.

Pigments

A complete list, a dictionary as it were, of pigments used in painting would fill a far larger volume than the present one. This is partly due to the fact that virtually every conceivable substance capable of tinting or colouring a surface, from insect juice to urine, has at some time or other been the subject of experiment by artists and partly because of the enormous number of synonyms. In addition there are names of pigments that are hard to identify or that may have never existed. For example, there was a pigment known in antiquity as dragon's blood, which is thought to have been a red resin used for the colouring of varnishes and coming from the East. Reference to this pigment is made by Pliny in the eighth book of his *Historia Naturalis*, where he speaks at length of the animosity between the elelphant and the dragon, telling us that they are constantly engaged in battle and how they both lose their lives on account of their being equally matched. The dragon wraps its deadly coils around the elephant, who when vanquished falls upon his fiery foe to crush him with his weight. Later on, in book XXXIII, the classical author informs his readers that the dense liquid that issues from the crushed dragon mixes with the blood of the dying elephant to produce a pigment that should rightly be called cinnabar (vermilion). Again in book XXXV, complaining of the excessive number and brilliance of the colours used by the Roman painters of his day compared to the austere palette of the older Greeks, Pliny remarks that the craze for so many pigments did not result in the production of fine works of art but rather in India being able to export the slime of her rivers (thought to be a reference to indigo) and the putrid blood of her elephants and dragons.

Dragon's blood was known, at least by name, by our old friend Cennino Cennini, whose enthusiasm for it seems to have been limited.

> A colour known as dragon's blood is red. This colour is used occasionally on parchment for illuminating. But leave it alone and do not have much respect for it, for it is not of a constitution to do you much credit.[33]

It will be understood from all this that even a short list of the relatively practical pigments could scarcely contain less than 500 entries. Luckily for us the Old Masters very wisely confined themselves to a few pigments, the properties of which they knew intimately, and it can be taken as axiomatic that a masterpiece can be produced with a very limited palette indeed. We are told, for instance, that two of the greatest artists of ancient Greece, Apelles and Nicomachus, used only four colours: chalk white, yellow ochre, red ochre and lamp black or charcoal black. An explanation of why only three colours – black, white and red – were sometimes chosen is contained in the technique of *à trois crayons* (*see* pp. 32–4).

The chemist A. P. Laurie, on studying a painting by Frans Hals (1581/5– 1666) entitled *Lady with a Fan* (National Gallery of Scotland, Edinburgh), discovered that it was yet again a picture painted with the same four colours as used by the ancients – white, yellow, red and black – with the addition of a few dabs of green, which might well be, in fact, a mixture of the black and yellow.

The palette of Hals and Rembrandt

The colours used by Frans Hals were:

1. Flake white
2. Yellow ochre
3. Red ochre (in the case of the Edinburgh portrait, scarlet lake)
4. Charcoal black

Rembrandt's palette must have been very similar to the above. Probably identical save for the addition of the siennas and the umbers, for the master loved the earth colours and called them those 'friendly' colours.

Titian is quoted by his pupil, Jacopo Palma Il Giovane (1544–1628), as saying a good painter needs only three colours. He practised what he preached. There is a portrait by the artist in the Galleria Borghese, Rome, that I believe to have been painted with no more. Certainly in his maturity his underpainting was carried out with only three colours: flake white, burnt sienna and ivory black.

These three colours are, in fact, contained in Titian's palette as reconstructed by Maurice Busset,[34] which I give with the comment that while the artist certainly used these pigments throughout his long working life, he sometimes used less and sometimes more. Where, for instance, is the Venetian red that is so often recognized in his work? Unless of course it is the red ochre.

Titian's palette

1. Flake white
2. Genuine ultramarine
3. Madder lake
4. Burnt sienna
5. Malachite
6. Yellow ochre
6. Red ochre
8. Orpiment
9. Ivory black

Rubens' palette

Busset has also reconstructed the palette of Rubens. I give it with the same reservations that I express for that of Titian.

1. Flake white
2. Orpiment
3. Yellow ochre
4. Yellow lake
5. Madder
6. Vermilion
7. Red ochre
8. Genuine ultramarine
9. Azur d'Allemagne
10. Terre verte
11. Vert azur
12. Malachite green
13. Burnt sienna
14. Ivory black

An examination of the contents of a trunk deposited in the Rubenshuis Museum, Antwerp, containing powdered colours employed in the studio of Rubens, has shown that all those pigments that we also find on one or other or all of the reconstructed palettes of Apelles, Titian, Hals and Rembrandt – flake white, genuine ultramarine, the madders and the earth colours – are in good condition. Whereas those colours that the Antwerp master has added to the list, the yellow lake, the vermilion and the vegetable greens have, we are told, faded almost entirely away.

A careful study of the above lists allows us to begin to construct a basic forger's palette containing no colour that was not known to the Old Masters. All are durable, and each one is obtainable today. Such a palette would contain ten colours – six more than we would need if we had the ability of an Apelles or a Hals. They are:

1. Flake white	6. Raw umber
2. Yellow ochre	7. Burnt umber
3. Red ochre	8. Terre verte
4. Raw sienna	9. Genuine ultramarine
5. Burnt sienna	10. Ivory black

To this list we may safely add, as needs arise, any variety of earth colour: for instance, brown ochre, Pozzuoli red, Indian and Venetian red, as well as bone black, vine black, lamp black, etc. All we need to complete our palette are a strong yellow and red. By 'strong' I do not intend the colour's covering power but its prismic brightness. In the Old Master palettes set out above, the strong bright yellow is orpiment (arsenic trisulphide). This pigment is no longer in commerce. The reason for it being obsolete may be summed up thus: it is not durable, it mixes badly, and it is a deadly poison. Its defects were well known by the Old Masters themselves, and writing in the sixteenth century Cornelius Jansen says: 'Orpiment will ly fayre on any colour except verdigris but no colour can ly fayre on him; he kills them all.'[35] Even T. De Mayerne, a physician in the court of Charles I, speaking of van Dyck, says: 'He makes use of orpiment, which is the finest yellow to be found', but has to qualify his praise with: 'But it dries very slowly and when mixed with other colours, it destroys them.'[36] Van Dyck's secret for using orpiment successfully was to apply it unmixed on areas of drapery that had already been underpainted with other yellows. It is amazing how a whole area of relatively dull yellow such as yellow ochre can be made brilliant with just a well-placed touch or two of brighter yellow. The modern version of orpiment, sometimes known as king's yellow, is composed of a mixture of chrome yellow and zinc white, both of which we may only use in our decorative fakes. So for the perfect fake we either have to go to the ridiculous length of preparing it ourselves, at which point we might as well start weaving our own canvas or take the simpler course of not painting a picture that perforce needs orpiment. Or, if you really can't finish your painting without a bright yellow, damage the area where the orpiment should be and then skilfully retouch the damage with the modern chrome yellow and zinc- or flake-white mixture.

We have no serious problem in obtaining a strong red for, in spite of it having 'faded' along with the fugitive colours from Rubens' studio, vermilion is perfectly acceptable. The colour was known in medieval times and is perfectly durable if carefully prepared and properly used. Our galleries are hung with hundreds of Old Master paintings containing well-preserved vermilion.

Theoretically we should also be able to employ madder. Unfortunately, however, genuine madder, the product of the madder root, is very difficult to obtain. The discovery in the nineteenth century of the colouring principles of madder – alizarin and purpurin – and the subsequent production of synthetic madder, has led to the virtual cessation of its manufacture. Chemically speaking, a really good artificially produced madder should not differ from the real thing. Therefore, if you must have madder buy it from a first-class colour merchant and ask them what is in it. But personally I think there is no red in the Old Masters that we cannot simulate with the colours now at our disposal, and I shall not add it to the forger's list of pigments. Our forger's palette now looks like this.

The forger's palette

1. Lead (flake) white
2. Yellow ochre
3. Chrome yellow[a]
4. Raw sienna
5. Red ochre
6. Burnt sienna
7. Vermilion
8. Raw umber
9. Burnt umber
10. Terre verte
11. Genuine ultramarine[b]
12. Ivory black[c]

[a] For decorative fakes only.
[b] May be exchanged for good cobalt blue for decorative fakes (*see below* under lapis lazuli).
[c] Lamp black or charcoal black may be used if preferred.

If you are to learn to use these colours to the greatest effect you must know their properties and how to prepare them. To this end, let us discuss them one by one.

1. LEAD (FLAKE) WHITE

This pigment has many other names, the most used being Cremnitz white and blanc d'argent. It is traditionally made by exposing lead plates to the fumes of vinegar, which causes a white scum – carbonate of lead – to form on them. The pigment prepared from this is toxic and for this reason has largely been replaced in the art supply shops by other whites, such as titanium and zinc.

2. YELLOW OCHRE

This colour is known under various names: Roman ochre, golden ochre, Oxford ochre, brown ochre, ochre jaune, etc. The long list of names applied to the colour is due to the fact that it is a natural earth colour, existing in many places and in differing qualities, varying much in colour and, to some extent, in chemical composition. It has been used since earliest times, is absolutely durable and may be mixed in safety with any of our other colours. For our use we need the brightest (not lightest) ochre we can find. It should be bought in powder form and, before grinding, heated up to a temperature a little below that of boiling water. This is because it has a tendency to absorb moisture from air, which is undesirable in oil paint. You are strongly advised to search thoroughly for the best quality. And since the colour is often insufficiently washed it is advisable to wash it again – a process that results in a colour of the greatest beauty.

3. CHROME YELLOW

This is a chromate of lead or a chromate and sulphate of lead, depending on its shade. Cadmium yellow should replace chrome yellow where permanence is a consideration. As mentioned elsewhere, chrome yellow is for decorative work only, as, indeed, cadmium yellow must be.

4. RAW SIENNA

This colour gets its name from the town in Italy, Siena, where it is mined. It is absolutely reliable, and, being in effect a dark, rich yellow ochre together with a good bright ochre, it provides us with a fine range. It all depends, however, on the quality. If our yellow ochre and our raw sienna are too alike (and they can be virtually identical), then clearly there is no advantage in having both on our palette. Again it is a matter of shopping around for the right variety.

5. RED OCHRE

Mostly known as light red, this colour is calcined, light yellow ochre. Curiously, the best yellow ochre does not produce the best red ochre. Here again you must look around for a fine quality. It has all the virtues of yellow ochre.

6. BURNT SIENNA

This, as its name tells us, is calcined raw sienna. Sienna, both burnt and raw, varies considerably according to the vein of earth from which it is mined; what we are looking for in our burnt sienna is a richness and a depth of colour. When mixed with oil it appears as a reddish brown and is often classified as a brown, but it is as both a brown and a red that it is useful to us. Its red property only becomes apparent when it is used as a glaze over lighter colours. Skilfully employed, it produces one of the most attractive reds at our disposal.

7. VERMILION (CINNABAR)

Cinnabar, or sulphide of mercury, is one of the commonest ores and was probably first used to prepare pigment in its natural form. But a finer colour is produced artificially. Artificial vermilion was almost certainly known in the time of Theophrastus (372–287BC), who describes the preparation of mercury. Cennino Cennini seems to have been acquainted with the artificial variety, as he writes: 'This colour is produced by Alchemy, performed in an Alembic...you may find recipes among the friars.'[37] The alchemy he speaks of is performed by subliming sulphur and mercury in a covered crucible. The vermilion forms in crystalline masses at the top.

The finest product comes from China, where it has long been considered a royal colour. Marco Polo tells us that the signature of Kublai Khan, the Mongol emperor of China, was stamped on his paper currency in vermilion. The Chinese product is, however, difficult to obtain, and you must beware of imitations for it is rumoured that some European manufacturers wrap their poor quality vermilion in Chinese paper.

8. RAW UMBER

Raw umber is an oxide and hydrate of iron and manganese. It should be heated up before grinding with oil. It is absolutely stable. Again, quality varies enormously. Personally I am fond of umber with a very definite greenish tint about it as this contrasts well with the warmer burnt umber, while maintaining a family likeness; thus we have unity in variety. In fact, all earths may be considered as a family in harmony.

9. BURNT UMBER

As its name suggests, it is calcined, raw umber. Some have disputed its stability, but there seems to be no real grounds for doubting that it is an absolutely permanent colour.

10. TERRE VERTE (GREEN EARTH)

A transparent colour, lacking body, but if properly underpainted it can produce a most attractive colour. It was used by Canaletto (1697–1768) with blue and yellow ochre to reproduce the limpid colour of Venetian canals as they were in his day. Perhaps in our time we might try cow dung.

11. GENUINE ULTRAMARINE (LAPIS LAZULI)

'Ultramarine blue is a colour noble, beautiful and perfect beyond all other colours, and there is nothing that can be said of it but it will yet exceed this praise.'[38] So Cennino Cennini lauds the most famous of all blues, real ultramarine. Endless trouble was once expended on its preparation, and consequently it has always been a costly pigment. The artists of Cennini's time, working for the Church, got their supply from the monasteries, numbers of which were famous for preparing it. The monks prized it as highly as the painters, and there are many tales of how parsimonious they were with it and how they suspected (probably with good reason) the artists of stealing it. For a detailed account of its preparation in those days the reader is referred to Cennini's *Il libro dell'arte*. Genuine ultramarine is still prepared to this day, but it is terribly expensive. I have recently bought enough to make a small tube of it at a price of £250 – so we can only afford to use it on work of the utmost importance. For our decorative fakes we must content ourselves with the artificial ultramarine or cobalt blue. Oddly enough, it is the best cobalt, not ultramarine, that comes closest to the real thing in appearance. You must, however, be sure to buy only the very best-quality cobalt. The inferior varieties are treacherous in mixtures. A simple test of quality is to mix a little of the blue with burnt sienna and white; if the result is greenish it is not suitable. It may be significant that the good-quality cobalt, which turns the mixture with burnt sienna and white towards the mauve side, usually costs little more than the inferior variety, but the slight difference in price does not reflect the vast difference in quality.

12. IVORY BLACK

Like all blacks, it is a stable colour. It tends towards blue, and, if surrounded by warm-enough colours and mixed with white, it can, by a good painter, be made to look like that colour. Bone black, vine black, charcoal black, etc., all made by burning different substances, may be substituted for ivory black, as need arises. They all have their own virtues, which experience will teach you to recognize.

A General Note on Binding Media

We now have at our disposal not only traditional supports with good and appropriate grounds, or primings, but also a fine set of pigments that, unless stated otherwise, were all known and employed by the Old Masters. And these last, being found in nature, have precisely the same chemical structure as those used in painting from the earliest times. We may rely on them to stand up to the scrutiny of scientific examination.

But even so, we still have no paints, for pigment only becomes paint when it is mixed with some liquid or other that will hold it together. This is, of course, why we call these various liquids binding media. It is the binding medium that determines whether the Old Master we are to paint is going to be a tempera or an oil painting or whatever. There are several other types of paintings such as fresco, encaustic and watercolour, together with many mixed media, but in these pages we shall speak only of the basic techniques of tempera, by which is intended egg tempera, and oil. These two techniques mastered, we will have no difficulty emulating any easel picture (at least from the technical standpoint) that may strike our fancy, and learn to combine these techniques as need arises. This being so, before discussing any particular binding medium it might be as well to give a general outline first of the tempera and then of the oil techniques.

Egg Tempera

This ancient method of painting has many advantages and beauties. One is its great colour range. R. Spencer Stanhope says of it:

> 'There is no medium of any kind in use in painting which so little, if at all, affects the colours with which it is mixed. It leaves them their soft effect, permanence and brilliance. It dries at once, and the colour never changes. It leaves a perfect surface with no brushmarks, and the painting may be looked at in any light.'[39]

Support for tempera

The ideal support for tempera is panel, and, in fact, the masters you will be following in this technique will mostly be the early Italian artists of the fourteenth and fifteenth centuries who painted before the general employment of canvas. Icons should also be painted in tempera and later varnished. Not, as many fakers do, painted in oil.

The ground for tempera

The ground will be the gesso ground of Cennino Cennini (*see* pp. 82–4). If you have any trouble with getting the paint to work well on it, you may try rubbing it over with garlic.

The preparatory drawing

A thorough preparatory drawing is an essential for tempera painting, for unlike oil painting it does not allow constant correction without losing some of its freshness of colour. The preparatory drawing may be transferred to the panel either by pouncing or by squaring.

POUNCING

Pouncing is carried out thus. The lines are first perforated with a pin or needle, and then finely powdered charcoal is pounced through them. This is done by putting the charcoal dust into a coarse muslin bag, which is dabbed forcibly on to a drawing that has been taped to the panel. The charcoal is thus forced through the perforations to make a drawing of dotted lines on the ground. This drawing is gone over with a brush or pen with a light paint or ink, and after this has dried the charcoal is brushed away. Plates 26 and 27 illustrate a drawing pricked for pouncing by Gianfrancesco Penni: (1496–1528) and my copy of it, which is not pricked.

SQUARING

Squaring is a simple process and has the advantage over pouncing of being able to enlarge or reduce any given drawing. Many Old Master drawings have come down to us squared for transfer, and we should study them well. When the design is complicated, and many squares have been used, then the squares should be numbered to avoid confusion.

To enlarge or reduce a rectangle to one of the same proportion, one merely has to draw a diagonal through it and two new sides that meet on the diagonal.

UNDERDRAWING

The drawing on the panel should be as complete as you can make it for this will save you endless trouble later on. A splendid example of the kind of drawing that must lie below the surface of many early panel pictures is Jan van Eyck's (active 1422–41) *St Barbara* in the Koninklijk Museum voor Schone Kunsten, Antwerp. This picture reveals exactly the same method as that proposed by Cennino Cennini, who tells us that when we are replacing our charcoal drawing with a brush charged with ink we must also put in the shadows. And in van Eyck's picture we see it completed in so far as light and shade and the colouring of the sky just begun (*see* plate 28).

Among other unfinished panel paintings to come down to us is Michelangelo's *Entombment* in the National Gallery, London. Here again we see the enormous care that the Old Masters took in their underdrawing and painting. This was not because they had time to waste, quite the opposite. They knew that by building a sound foundation much time would be saved at a later stage. The *Entombment* shows us the stage after the preliminary drawing and before the final layer, which would probably have consisted mostly of oil glazes.

Another unfinished painting in the National Gallery, London, attributed to Michelangelo and known as *The Manchester Madonna* is also very instructive. This shows the underpainting of the flesh carried out in terre verte, a practice that seems to have been introduced, or at least made popular, by Giotto (*c.*1267–1337) and continued spasmodically right up until G. B. Tiepolo (1696–1770) in the eighteenth century and still finds practitioners in certain quarters even today. Incidentally the attribution of these two paintings to Michelangelo has been questioned, but no scholar has come up with a convincing alternative; perhaps they are the work of a Renaissance colleague of ours. If so, well done!

But to return to painting in tempera. We have arrived at the stage of a finished drawing on a pure-white ground and are preparing to set to work and paint. This is the moment when we must mix our pigments (freshly every day) with our binding media containing egg and so produce our paint.

How to prepare egg tempera

The binding part of the egg is the yolk. This simple fact would seem to have been kept a close secret, at least from painters, and I have seen a number of modern flaking panels and canvases where some innocent soul has thrown away the yolk and painted with the white. The yolk of the egg may be mixed with your pigments with no addition beyond a little water to arrive at a consistency suitable for painting. Cennino Cennini recommends the mixture of yolk and pigment in equal parts, presumably by volume. The pigment should be worked up to a stiff paste with water first, and then the egg worked in very conscientiously indeed so that it is evenly distributed throughout the mix. This mixing is done with either a spatula or a palette-knife on a thick sheet of glass. Actual grinding of the pigment by hand is no longer necessary as we can buy them already ground, sometimes more finely than the Old Masters could manage (a situation we may have to correct, as will be explained in Chapter 10).

Some authorities recommend using the whole egg. The white really has the property of a glue and must not be used alone to mix colours as they will certainly flake. Others suggest a little of the white combined with the yolk to add translucency. Some old recipes advocate the addition of vinegar and oil. The following recipe is taken from Hilaire Hiler,[40] who tells us that it was traditionally used by a branch of the Benedictine Order in the little town of Beuron, Germany, for application on a gesso ground. It is supplied by Father Paulinus.

Father Paulinus's medium for egg tempera

1. Whisk the whites and yolks of 4 eggs well together.
2. Mix together 1 tablespoon of boiled linseed oil with 1 teaspoon of vinegar.

3. Combine the two mixtures and shake them up thoroughly.

4. Strain through muslin to remove skins, and bottle until needed.

When the medium is mixed with the colours, water is used to thin the paint to the required consistency.

This recipe is really an emulsion and brings us to a classic egg-yolk and linseed emulsion that requires the same skill as is needed for making home-made mayonnaise, a skill, folklore has it, most easily acquired by pregnant women. And if you are working in the kitchen no one will suspect for a moment what you are really up to, but I don't advise anyone to taste the result.

Egg tempera with linseed oil

1. Separate the yolk from the white of six eggs. The best method is the way used by most cooks: crack the eggs on the edge of a pan or bowl, as if you were about to fry them, and then let the white drain off through the crack as much as it will. This done, separate the shell into two halves and pass the yolk from one half to the other, pouring off the remaining white as you do so.

2. Take 10 drops of oil of lavender for each yolk, and add this to the yolks very slowly, drop by drop, beating all the time with a fork.

3. Put a small quantity of this egg and lavender-oil mixture into a suitable receptacle, and beat in one drop of sun-bleached linseed oil in the same way as you did with the lavender oil – that is slowly and thoroughly beating all the time. Continue alternating a drop of the egg mixture and a drop of oil until you have what Tudor-Hartt calls: 'a stiff, butter-coloured mayonnaise'.[41]

This 'mayonnaise' is now ready to mix with pigment to produce paint. The pigment is first mixed with water to form a thick paste. This process is carried out with a palette-knife on the sheet of plate-glass mentioned above. The medium is then added to the pigment paste in equal parts, as measured by volume, and very thoroughly mixed together to form a smooth paint. A few drops of water are sprinkled on to the mixture from time to time to facilitate the grinding.

To use this emulsion for diluting paint for application, it is combined with an equal volume of water, which is added in the following way. The medium is put on the grinding-slab as a blob, an indentation is made in the centre and filled with about a tablespoon of water, which is gradually worked in until the mixture is thin enough to run off the palette-knife. The thinned medium is then put into a suitable container, and the remainder of the water stirred in. Incidentally, the palette used for mixing one's colours for tempera painting should, like that used for watercolour painting, be non-absorbent.

To sum up the technique of painting in tempera:

1. The best support is panel.
2. The best ground is gesso.
3. The simplest and possibly the best way of preparing your paints is first to grind your pigments to a paste in water and then to mix them with egg-yolk in approximately equal parts by volume, as recommended by Cennini. To test whether or not you have put too much or too little egg in your paint, paint the sample to be tested out on the palette, let it dry and moisten a part of it. If there is no difference in tone between the dry and the moistened part then it is as it should be. A further test is to scrape off a sliver of the dried paint with a palette-knife: if it flakes there is too much egg, and you must add more pigment; if it crumbles there is not enough yolk. But if it comes off as a greasy sliver you may leave it as it is.

In spite of the fun of making mayonnaise, it has not been shown that any addition to the yolk of egg is necessary; the common inclusion of vinegar, to be found in many old recipes, is positively harmful to genuine ultramarine.

Oil Painting

Much of what has been said about tempera painting applies equally well to oil painting. Here, again, is the need for a pure-white ground. Indeed there is a greater need for the ground to be as white as possible because the oil binding yellows and darkens the colours far more than the egg-yolk medium, which seems to remain virtually unchanged. It has already been explained how, as the oil darkens with age, it gains in translucency, so that more and more of the light from the white ground is refracted through it and, to a certain extent, compensates for the lowering of tone.

Then, again, as with tempera, there is the need for careful preparatory drawings so that the colours may be laid on with confidence in the right place from the start, so saving time with later corrections, which tend to muddy the colours. It was not, however, the custom of the Old Masters to make modelli for oil painting – that is, highly finished preparatory drawings of the whole composition – as is necessary for tempera, unless it was to show a patron what the completed work would be like. Normally the preparatory drawings were of two kinds: the compositional sketch, which was often dashed off with the greatest freedom and economy, and the study, usually from life of some detail. These preparatory drawings were then used to make a complete drawing in charcoal on the canvas itself. Upon this drawing the masters painted their underpainting, which was frequently monochrome, and then their final painting, glazes and varnishes.

The principle behind this traditional method is this. The subject to be painted is conceived of as possessing three qualities: outline, tone and colour. As we all know, none of these three things actually exists in nature; they are concepts, very useful concepts, that nevertheless have no reality outside of ourselves. The theory of Impressionism has its basis in the fact that what we actually experience of any object of sight is the light reflected from it, and in that light the qualities of outline, tone and colour are inseparable, save by an act of conscious or subconscious thought. So the Impressionist painter decided that each brushstroke of paint would be mixed to the desired tone and colour and put in the right place without outlines all in one operation. This clearly requires immense skill and knowledge, and a number of Impressionists rose to the challenge and created some very fine pictures. But every gain in art is accompanied by a corresponding loss, which incidentally, is why, unlike science, there is no progress in art. Whereas we expect the modern scientist to know more of physics than the alchemist of old, we do not expect the modern artist to know more of art than his predecessors or a Picasso to be 'better' than a Giotto. In this lies the timelessness of our occupation.

But to return to the Impressionist method of putting down in one stroke what the Old Masters led up to through different stages. What exactly was sacrificed by abandoning the traditional methods of the former masters? Well, the first thing to be lost was having the possibility of tackling the three aesthetic issues of linear design, tonal design and colour scheme in three distinct operations. The problems of linear design were solved by the earlier artists at the stage of the completed drawing, whether that drawing was made separately or directly on the canvas; the tonal design was completed at the stage of the monochrome underpainting; and the colour design worked out at the final stages. This allowed for the maximum concentration on each of these artistic points individually, without being in the least distracted by the others. Naturally this led to a very high standard in all three, and the linear and tonal designs of the best Old Masters remain unsurpassed by the Impressionists and Post-Impressionists. They might, on occasion, however, outdo the Old Masters in regard to certain aspects of colour, the most obvious being to create local colour in the shadows in place of the shades of brown that are so common in the older oil paintings. The greatest loss to painting brought about by the Impressionist movement, lies, however, in the loss of the picture's quality as an object.

Pictures are not, as some people think, images of something else but are themselves something. In other words, they do not express an idea; they are the idea. And just as a poem cannot be separated from its words, because the words are the poem, nor can a picture be separated from the materials of which it is composed. It was an awareness of this truth that gave rise to Robert Frost's much quoted definition of poetry as 'that which gets lost in translation', and we may similarly define painting as that which gets lost in reproduction.

This brings us back to the point made in the previous chapter: copies and reproductions of Old Master paintings that confine themselves to imitating only the surface colour are missing out all the painterly and tactile values of the work. They are neglecting the scumbles, the glazes, the impasto and all the rest of the masterly handling that goes into the making of the beautifully painted object that an oil painting should be. These qualities that are lost to modern art must be rediscovered by the diligent forger who wishes to convince in his or her efforts to work in the manner of the Old Masters.

So let us now discuss the properties of the principal oils and varnishes used by the old painters for binding their pigments, for these determine many properties of the resultant paint – its gloss, its transparency, its consistency and much else.

Nut oil

Nut oil is very light in colour. It is not quite as good a dryer as linseed oil and easily turns rancid, but nevertheless it was much used by the Old Masters. Vasari specifically states that walnut oil is better (than linseed oil) because it yellows less with time, which is not something that concerns us, although it was the principal oil of the seventeenth century and can still be obtained. Here, from *Leonardo on Painting* (ed. Martin Kemp, New Haven and London, 1989), is Leonardo's recipe for nut oil:

> Select the finest walnuts: take them from their shell; soak them in a glass vessel, in clear water, till you can remove the rind. Then replace the substance of the nut in clear water, changing the latter as often as it becomes turbid, six or even eight times. After some time, the nuts on being stirred, separate and become decomposed of themselves, forming a solution like milk. Expose this in plates to the open air, and the oil will float on the surface.

It is said that a mixture of linseed oil and poppy oil in equal parts has the same properties as nut oil.

Linseed oil

This is the oil that is of the greatest use to us. It is easily obtainable and in various qualities. It comes from the seeds of the flax plant, which is the same plant that supplies us with the fibre with which our linen canvases are made. The various qualities of linseed oil now follow.

COLD PRESSED

The linseed oil to be bought off the shelf is seldom cold pressed because this method of extracting the oil from the seed gives the smallest yield. Nevertheless it is obtainable, at a price, from some of the more conscientious suppliers. The best variety is a clear, golden yellow that does not become cloudy or thicken quickly when subjected to cold.

HOT PRESSED

This oil is in every way inferior to the cold-pressed variety: it is cloudier; it does not flow as well from the brush; and it does not dry through properly (easily forming a wrinkled skin). In short, have nothing to do with it.

BLEACHED

Linseed oil is sometimes bleached to remove its yellowness. In the past the most common method was to put it in covered glass jars in the sun. After a few weeks the oil will be clear, sometimes as limpid as water, but it is a temporary change, and the oil will shortly revert to its former colour. There are many other bleaching processes such as heating with fuller's earth, or adding certain chemicals, all of which are as unsatisfactory as they are unnecessary. So, again, we need have nothing to do with it.

PURIFIED

Purified linseed oil is certainly advantageous to the painter as purification improves the drying power. The cold-pressed oil of commerce is usually purified. If, however, you wish to do it yourself, you may follow Dürer's method of filtering the oil through fine, powdered charcoal. Alternatively, just let the oil stand until the impurities have sunk to the bottom. For those who like to make work for themselves, here is a method given by Philippe Nuñez of Lisbon:

> To purify linseed oil for the whites and the blues, take a vessel having an orifice at the bottom (a bottle turned upside down will do), which may be stopped and unstopped. Throw in the oil mixed with spring water, and, after stirring well, let the mixture settle till the oil remains uppermost; then gently remove the stopper, letting out the water, and as soon as the oil begins to come out, stop the orifice. Do this three or four times, and the oil will be very clear and fit for use.[42]

Any water left in the oil may be removed by adding a lump of quicklime.

STAND OIL

This oil is a must for the faker. It was extensively used by the Old Masters, and a good quality one can be readily purchased in the art shops. It is produced by heating linseed oil, as far as possible in the absence of air, until it thickens. During this process the molecules group themselves together to form larger ones, which are chemically more stable. The earliest recipe for stand oil comes from Heraclius, a Roman writer of the thirteenth century. This oil is too thick and sticky for grinding pigments unless it is combined with linseed oil in its normal state or thinned with turpentine. It was almost certainly used by the earliest painters in oil, and with proper usage it can produce much crisper edges than ordinary linseed oil. For this reason it is, or until recently was, much used by sign-writers, among whom a number of the Old Master's workshop secrets survive.

BOILED OIL

Stand oil is a form of boiled oil. As traditionally prepared in Holland, it is boiled for six to eight hours at 290°C (554°F). But the boiled oil sold on the market as such is produced by a slight boiling with a considerable amount of dryers, and the resulting oil is unsuitable for good work.

Poppy oil

This oil has two purposes: it can retard drying, and, because it is colourless, it may be used to grind delicate blues when there is a fear of sullying the colour with a yellow oil. Neither of these considerations is normally any concern of ours. The fact that it dries slowly is really a great disadvantage because mixed with some pigment it can take years to dry through, and we don't want to get caught red- (or perhaps it was blue-) handed, as Elmyr de Hory once was, offering a still-wet masterpiece for sale.

Oil of spike and lavender

Both these oils are slow drying, and they are sometimes used by colour-merchants to retard the drying of paints made up in tubes. But we have no use for them. On the rare occasions when we may find a role for a slow-drying oil, poppy oil is preferable.

Examining the above list of oils it will be clear that linseed oil is the only one that need really concern us. It can do everything that nut oil can do with none of the disadvantages, and we may now consider how it is to be ground with pigments.

Grinding oil colours

As I have suggested elsewhere, 'grinding', as applied to preparing paint from our already well-ground pigments, should really be called 'mixing'. All the physical effort of grinding lumps of pigment to powder by hand has been spared us, but as forgers are nothing if not traditionalists I shall still use 'grinding' interchangeably with 'mixing'.

The equipment necessary for grinding oil colours is precisely the same as that used for mixing tempera colours: the slab of non-porous stone – or, more conveniently, a thick sheet of glass – a spatula or palette-knife and a muller. The main difference between grinding oil colours and tempera colours is that whereas for tempera the pigments are first ground to a paste with water, the pigment used for oil colours must be completely dry. To this end it is sometimes necessary to heat them before grinding. The method of grinding is well set out by Max Doerner:

> At the beginning of the grinding but very little oil is added to the pigment powder and these are first mixed together with the spatula or a broad palette knife. The colour thus made into a paste is deposited in an upper corner of the slab. A little of it at a time, as much as the size of a walnut, is then ground with a circular motion, under slight pressure, and spread gradually over the whole surface of the slab. After this the colour is heaped up, the runner 'the muller' is scraped off and the grinding repeated, if necessary. The colour, which may have seemed a little dry at the start, will now flow more easily. One should guard against 'pouring' oil on dry pigments. If the colour is too thin, more dry pigment is added. Artists' pigments should be ground to the consistency of paste so that they 'stand up' and do not run like house-painter's paint. The finished colour is deposited in another corner of the slab. The colour, while being ground, should not make a crunching sound under the runner. Finally the whole batch is briefly given a last grinding. It is practical to grind first the light colours, beginning with white. Extreme caution is advised here, as with all poisonous lead colours; by tying a damp cloth over the nose and mouth one can avoid breathing in the white pigment dust.[43]

THE PROPORTION OF OIL TO PIGMENT

The following chart, based on Professor A. P. Laurie's findings, offers a very rough guide, but practice is a better one. The table below represents the approximate percentage by volume contained in the paints of our forger's palette. But figures for the requirements of oil in the manufacture of paint vary to a very marked degree from authority to authority.

Pigment	Oil (%)	Pigment	Oil (%)
Flake white	50	Vermilion	60
Yellow ochre	62	Raw umber	68
Chrome yellow	68	Burnt umber	72
Raw sienna	84	Terre verte	70
Red ochre	62	Ultramarine	54
Burnt sienna	86	Ivory black	70

Resins and varnishes

To the basic oil medium many of the Old Masters added a resin. The resins useful to us are only three in number and are all of natural origin: amber, copal and mastic. Of these only amber and copal may be used in the medium itself. Mastic is more useful for the final varnish, of which we shall speak when discussing how to give the appearance of age to a picture. When used, the resin should be evenly mixed throughout the paint and only applied in the upper layers of the painting. A good all-round varnish medium that I have myself used is as follows:

Turpentine	2 parts
Linseed oil	2 parts
Stand oil	3 parts
Oil copal varnish	2 parts

The ingredients are shaken together before use.

Naturally we have to vary our medium according to the artists in whose manner we are working, and no one medium will do for all. Constant experiment is necessary, but don't waste time practising with materials and methods the Old Masters never employed. Remember their natural materials were few, and their so-called 'secrets' were simple skills, patiently cultivated over years of application, which allowed them to get out of a handful of earths and one or two oils and varnishes the most extraordinary variety of colour and texture. Elbow grease was one of their main ingredients, for as the old adage goes: 'Genius is one per cent inspiration and ninety-nine per cent perspiration.'

The oils and varnishes listed above that were known and used by the Old Masters are all satisfactorily prepared by the better colour-merchants of today and easily procurable. Two major items alone are now lacking from our equipment: vehicles and brushes.

Vehicles

When speaking of painting, 'vehicle' is often used as though it were synonymous with 'medium'. It is simply a matter of usage. Personally, what I intend by vehicle is the liquid that we combine with our paint to thin it to the desired consistency for actual painting. This may, in fact, be identical with the binding medium. But as our own paint normally has quite enough oil and varnish in it, further thinning is usually carried out with the addition of a volatile liquid that will leave the paint with no more oil and varnish than when it left the grinding-slab, indeed sometimes considerably less. The paint and vehicle are mixed together on the palette with a brush. The vehicle most used by the painters of the past was turpentine.

TURPENTINE

Turpentine, or oil of turpentine, is what is known as an essential oil, that is to say, unlike the fatty oils – such as nut and linseed – it evaporates almost entirely. A test for its purity is to put a drop on a white sheet of paper, on which it should leave no permanent grease-stain. For the painter it is by far the best and most important of the essential oils. It is prepared from the resin of various pine trees, and its pleasant aromatic odour brings into the studio some of the olfactory joys of the forests whence it comes. Turpentine is only used as a vehicle alone in the underpainting. This is because of the general rule, formulated by Rubens and of the greatest importance, that we must paint fat over lean. The fatty oils should be more in the upper layers of the picture than in the lower.

Turpentine is a solvent and may be used to clean brushes and to remove spots of unwanted paint. And precisely because it is a solvent it must be used on a thoroughly dry ground, otherwise it will mix the colours of the underpainting with the white of the ground, destroying the latter's all-important brightness. Equally, before using it as a vehicle in the upper layers, the underpainting must be completely dry.

PETROL

Essence of petroleum is sometimes used as a vehicle when for some reason rapidity of drying is a consideration.

There are also very many other essences that are used by painters, but no vehicle other than turpentine needs really to concern us here.

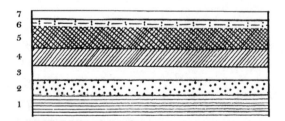

7. Final varnish or varnishes
6. Glazes for adjusting chromatic effects
5. Polychrome final painting
4. Monochrome underpainting
3. Complete drawing
2. Size
1. Canvas

Diagram of a vertical section through a complex Old Master painting such as a late Titian

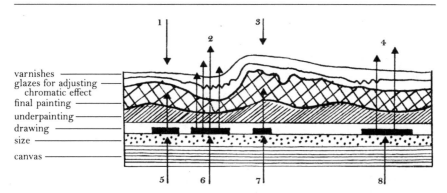

The same section indicating how the different layers of paint of varying thickness influence the refraction of the light from within the white ground   1. Impasto of medium thickness in the clear zones   2. Nuances in the mid-tones   3. Thicker impasto in the nuances   4. Thin glazes in the dark zones   5. The luminous ground is (quasi) diminished   6. The luminous ground is partially diminished to produce sombre effects   7. The luminous ground is diminished   8. The luminous ground appears relatively unchanged

Brushes
Brushes may be divided into the soft and stiff varieties.

SOFT BRUSHES
Of soft brushes, red sable are the best, and the synthetic version of them on the market today seem to have all the virtues of the real thing without involving us in an enormous expenditure. There are other soft brushes, but since we must, in principle, only use the best, we need not waste time on them except for carrying out rough jobs, where the brush is used but once and thrown away.

STIFF BRUSHES
These are usually made of pig's bristle. They are obtainable in all sorts of shapes and sizes according to their uses. Round brushes were the ones chiefly used by the Old Masters. The brush represented in my copy of Brueghel's drawing (*see* plate 11) is as much a caricature as the connoisseur's face. No fine work could ever have been produced with such an article. It intentionally has all the faults of a bad brush. Although we cannot see its tip, it is clear that it is not strictly conical, its bristles seem to stand out, and one wonders whether or not it would end in any kind of acceptable point. Such a brush might be used for the broadest underpainting but nothing else. For, as

Delacroix (1798–1863) said, 'You may start with a broom, but you must end with a needle.' Nowadays we have excellent brushes from which to choose, and there is absolutely no reason to make one's own. For our work we need a great variety from broad, flat brushes, with which we may scumble (make a broken or stiffish layer of paint) with its side-on edge for linear work, to finely pointed sables for precise detail. A general rule is to use soft brushes on panel and stiff brushes on canvas, but simply do as the needs dictate.

As R. Topfer (1799–1846) rightly says:

One brush, no good for washes, is excellent for little touches; another, admirable for foliage, is deceptive for skies. From which it follows that there is no such thing as an absolutely good brush or an absolutely bad one – without mentioning the fact that the same brush, because of its caprice, is neither always excellent nor always detestable... One may nevertheless say that the principal conditions which characterise a good brush are its elasticity, which makes it straighten itself out naturally, a fine but soft point, a large enough 'belly' to contain water and strong enough to hold it suspended, so that the weight of its drop keeps the point wet. These qualities can only be obtained in brushes of medium size and – this is important – a little brush is bad for washes in Chinese ink for it produces work dry and without daring.[44]

This, of course, concerns watercolour brushes, but the same criteria holds good for soft brushes used in oil.

Now we are fully equipped to work except for minor but essential things such as palette, paint rags, a bottle of wine and a sense of humour. And in the next chapter we shall again be choosing an artist. Unless, of course, you are one of those fakers who allow the artist to choose them – in which case you will need a medium of quite another sort than those discussed above.

CHAPTER NINE

Forging Ahead

'His originality is to admit of none and yet he makes a kind of
masterpiece by producing poems whose substance is not his own
and each word of which is prescribed by a given text. I can hardly
refrain from claiming that the merit of so successfully completing
such a task is greater (as it is rarer) than that of an author entirely
free to choose his own means.'

PAUL VALÉRY

I n this chapter we are again to speak of borrowings, copies, variations, interpretations and adaptations along the lines of those we looked at in Chapter 4. We shall discuss examples of inspired and less inspired plagiarism that may perhaps assist us to forge ahead as best we may.

Some years back I was visiting the well-known art dealers, who specialize in Old Masters, P. & D. Colnaghi of Old Bond Street, London, in relation to some business we were doing together and had the pleasure of looking through their stock (one should always seize on every opportunity of looking at genuine Old Masters). Among the group of fine drawings I was shown were two drawings attributed to Claude Lorrain. One was a chalk drawing of a harbour scene with classical buildings, the other a study of cattle. The harbour scene was the larger and more important drawing and was priced at £9000 (to which we may add a nought to bring the price to today's equivalent). The study of cattle, however, was only a tenth of that price. Having made some money from the old firm, I thought I would spend some of it on the less important Claude and study it at home. Some months later business took me again to Colnaghi's, and I enquired about the more important Claude drawing.

'Oh that,' said the director to whom I was talking with disdain, 'that turned out to be a fake!'

Apparently it had been sold to an important American museum, which had detached it from its old mount only to discover that the drawing was on nineteenth-century paper rather than on the seventeenth-century sheet that they were expecting. The museum had returned the drawing, and Colnaghi's had given them their money back.

This story set me thinking. Who, I wondered, in the nineteenth century could have made such a drawing? It was not at all the over-finished kind of Claude imitation that was popular with the Victorians. It had all the signs of being a genuine preparatory, or working, drawing of very good quality. It could not, of course, be by Claude himself, but it must have been by somebody who knew a great deal about Claude's working methods. Suddenly I felt certain that I knew who the artist was. It was Claude's only serious rival, other than Poussin, in classical landscape painting: Turner. From 1800 Turner had deliberately imitated the French master on a number of occasions, but his most famous essay in the manner of Claude is a picture that he exhibited in 1815 at the Royal Academy, London: *Dido Building Carthage* (*see* plate 29). The artist was so proud of this imitation that he left it to the English nation on condition that it be hung in the National Gallery next to the Claude original (*see* plate 30). His wish was respected, and the picture is still there beside its prototype.

Claude was not the only artist whom Turner imitated. The Dutch marine painter Willem van de Velde the Younger (1633–1707) was also the subject of his imitative skills, this in spite of professing that he could never succeed. A contemporary writes: 'We were looking at van de Velde, and on someone observing, "I think you could go beyond that," he [Turner] shook his head and said, "I can't paint like him." '[45]

Now I am not sure that Colnaghi's drawing would be worth more money as a Turner than as a Claude, but I do know that a fake van de Velde by Turner is worth more than a genuine one of the same kind. In the summer of 1976 two pictures belonging to the Duke of Bridgewater were auctioned by Christie's: one was *The Approaching Storm* by van der Velde and the other was a pastiche painted by Turner to be a companion piece (*see* plates 31–2). The van de Velde realized £65,000, the Turner £340,000. So again we see that the name is everything. A fake by a 'good name' is more acceptable than a genuine work by a relatively minor one.

A way that we may take advantage of this situation now suggests itself. We know that Turner had many followers and imitators. This was largely due to the Victorian art critic John Ruskin's enthusiasm for Turner's work, which he advised artists and students to emulate. Ruskin himself was, incidentally, a very good imitator of Turner. Mentioned in Walter Thornbury's *Life* of the great painter as being influenced by Turner is, among a number of artists, the English painter William Etty (1787–1849), another good name. Although not as renowned as Turner, Etty holds a very respectable place in the history of British art as a painter of the nude. His handling of paint is not unlike that of Rubens. Although famous for his nudes, Etty did make other kinds of paintings, among which are a number of copies. Now what could be more natural than for Etty to have made a copy of a Turner when he came under the influence of that artist's colouring? This being so, let us suppose that on the back of my copy of Turner's famous *The Fighting Téméraire* (*see* plates 33 and 34) there was a discreet inscription attributing the work to Etty. Instead of it being a worthless copy it would suddenly stand a good chance of becoming a valuable example of Etty's abilities as a copyist. Then who knows how much it would be worth? I must try it.

To return to the theme of art into art, surely there is no artist more original than Goya (1747–1828). It is hard to imagine with his extraordinary gift for invention that he would have ever plagiarized the creations of other artists, especially those less talented than himself, yet the fact is that he did. One of his sources was the English sculptor John Flaxman (1755–1826). Between 1787 and 1794, Flaxman was enjoying the final years of what has been termed his 'Roman Holiday', when he was commissioned by a Mr Hope to illustrate Dante, Homer and Aeschylus. Mrs Flaxman told the diarist Henry Crabb-Robinson that the drawings were commissioned 'merely to furnish F with an occupation for the evenings'. The result of Flaxman's well-spent evenings resulted in what have come to be known as Flaxman's outlines. These outlines, for that is indeed all they are (*see* plates 35 and 36), had an enormous impact on the artists of his time. The reason for this is very hard for we of the twentieth century to understand. Sarah Symmons, to whose article in the *Burlington Magazine* of September 1976 I am indebted for my information on the subject, writes:

The illustrations might have not caused more than a ripple on the surface of early nineteenth-century classical research were it not for the fact that those vast pattern books of antique imagery, which were advocated by all teachers and radical theorists as being the only true source of a new style, were beyond the financial capacities of most young artists. Flaxman's little illustrations with their queer mixture of different sources and their archaic technique deriving from Greek vase painting were the most available compendium. Their bland, non-committal simplicity made them a series of formal exercises suggesting endless possibility. Accordingly in the nineteenth century they became an academic textbook for art students.[46]

'Academic textbook for art students'. What a notion! How that phrase grates on the modern ear. And, yet, what was the result of that academic textbook? Quite simply a few masterpieces by Goya, David (1748–1825), Ingres, William Blake (1757–1827), Pinelli and others. And this from a work that has suffered to all intents and purposes the fate predicted for it by W. B. Yeats in 1896. 'His [Flaxman's] designs to the *Divine Comedy* will be laid, one imagines, with some ceremony in that immortal wastepaper basket, in which Time carries with many sighs the failures of great men.'[47] It might well be worth the modern artists while to rummage through Time's wastepaper basket now and again.

Other copyists of the nineteenth century – Delacroix, Géricault (1791–1824) and Degas – are all noted for their originality. Delacroix's surviving copies of Rubens (*see* plates 37 and 38) and Raphael alone number somewhere in the region of a hundred, and Degas' extant copies come to at least 740. Most of the copies were made in the form of drawings, and although in this chapter we are really speaking of painting, we must never forget that fine drawing is the foundation of Old Master painting, and we should always work out our painted variations and copies in drawing first.

In 1895 the well-known collector Ludwig Mond acquired a most admirable fake in the manner of Francesco Francia (*c.*1450–1517/8). He bought it in Rome from the Spitover–Hass collection. Mond bequeathed this fine picture of the *Virgin and Child with an Angel* to the National Gallery, London, where it would still be admired to this day as an original Francia had it not been examined scientifically in 1955, when a number of observations led to its demotion. It is not a copy but a variant of an altarpiece painted by Francia for the church of the Misericordia in Bologna. Like the original it bore an inscription (now largely effaced) reading OPUS FRANCIAE AUR (EFIC) IS/ (M) CCCCLXXXV. The damning evidence furnished by the 1955 examination included the fact that, although the panel shows no signs of being cut down, the paint goes right up to the edges. This is unusual for panel pictures of the time that form altarpieces because these were normally painted *in situ* and already set into a frame, which, of course, covers the edges. More conclusive is the fact that the cracks on the Virgin's veil and elsewhere have been very skilfully painted in. Artistically, this fake sets us a very high standard indeed, although no doubt the experts can now detect something of the nineteenth century about it (hindsight has perfect vision). It is far better than many genuine old panel pictures that have come down to us from the fifteenth century.

As with drawings, so with paintings there have been a number of pastiches made by taking elements from different pictures and combining them into one. An example of one of the most curious is a picture where the faker has taken two female heads from two different masters. The profile behind it is copied from a Botticelli, *La Bella Simonetta*, in the Palazzo Pitti, Florence, and the nearer profile is after a portrait of a lady attributed to Piero del Pollaiuolo (1443–96) in the Poldi–Pezzoli museum in Milan (*see* plates 40, 41 and 42). This is not a very clever thing to do, except for decorative work, as the sources are too obvious. A more ingenious method is to paint a picture, the design of which is known only through old copies. Here, if you can improve on the quality of the old copies, your work may pass for the lost original. If not, it may yet be accepted as another interesting old replica.

One of the most shameful and, at the same time, shameless copies ever to be made, and one that could easily have damaged or destroyed the original was carried out by Abraham Wolfgang Küffner (1760–1817). In 1799 Küffner was lent, for the purpose of making a copy, a famous self-portrait by Dürer that had been owned ever since the sixteenth century by the municipality of Nuremberg. The lime-wood panel on which the portrait was painted was some 15mm (½in) thick. Thick enough, thought Küffner, for two pictures, so he set about sawing the panel in half to separate the front from the back. He then painted a copy of Dürer's picture on the front of the panel that had been formerly the back half of the original picture. As this section of the panel bore the seals and marks of identification, the copyist was able to return his copy in place of the original Dürer. This deception might have gone undetected for longer than it actually did, save for the fact that, some-time before 1805, Küffner sold the original to a certain lawyer, G. E. Petz, who, in turn, sold it for 600 gulden to the Elector of Bavaria for his collection at Munich. The Nuremberg Council got wind of this transaction and, comparing the picture in their possession with the Munich painting, realized what must have happened. They could not, however, annul the sale to Munich as it had been perfectly legal, and they were forced to live with their embarrassment, which is now on permanent loan to the house of Dürer. Curiously, they do not seem to have prosecuted Küffner for theft. He did, however, have a lengthy term of imprisonment in the castle of Rothenburg for coining. We are told that on his release he returned to Nuremberg, where he was, unaccountably, 'held in esteem'.

Here I would like to complete a story that I began in my autobiography, *Drawn to Trouble*, concerning a fragment of a painting from the workshop of the Bassano family of painters in the sixteenth century. The story began with buying pictures from an old couple who ran a curiosity shop in London. Louis and Marie were their names, and what I wrote was this:

Marie would sometimes take me to Louis' warehouse in Drury Lane, a once handsome Tudor building, then built around and dwarfed by later constructions which robbed it of light. The barn of a place was cheerless and uncared for, with small cracked and broken windows patched here and there with paper, as ineffective in keeping out the weather as they were of keeping out the thieves. Everything was broken down and ramshackle, but among the thousands of badly cared for paintings and prints the warehouse contained, were some of really fine quality. On one visit I noticed that most of the better paintings had a P chalked on the back of them. Marie told me that these pictures were reserved by an Italian dealer called Peretti. I had never met this dealer, but I knew him by reputation as a clever young man and he clearly had a good eye for paintings. It seemed to me, however, that it was unfair that he had earmarked all the best things in the warehouse so I took to surreptitiously rubbing out the P's on anything I particularly wanted. In this way I acquired a painting which has given me a great deal of pleasure over the years. It is a fragment of a painting by one of the Bassanos. The best of the Bassano family of painters was Jacopo [c.1517/8–92], and my painting representing the animals entering the ark known in several versions, may possibly have been designed by him and executed by Francesco [1549–92], one of his sons. Nobody can be certain. One can only judge by quality. So it is possible that some of Francesco's better work is given to Jacopo, and some of Jacopo's less good work attributed to Francesco or some other member of the family. But whether my picture is by one or both or neither of these artists does not matter to me in the least. Indeed, I am glad of the uncertainty, for if it were possible to give my Bassano a firm attribution, even as a fragment it would be too valuable for me to own. My enjoyment of it would be marred by such considerations as fearing it might be stolen, or wondering whether I had it sufficiently well insured. In short, I would have bought as much a problem as a pleasure.[48]

Since writing the above account, the picture has taken on an entirely different look, and perhaps I should explain how this came about. The fragment that I bought would appear to be exactly half of the original painting (*see* plate 43), the right-hand side of a composition that, as I mention above, comes from the Bassano family workshop. The first version of the *The Animals Entering the Ark* was painted about 1570 and is now in the Prado, Madrid (*see* plate 49). Tradition has it that it once belonged to Titian, who sold it to the Spanish Royal Collections. The Italian painter, etcher and art historian Carlo Ridolfi (1594–1658) says that Titian held the painting of the animals in high esteem and paid 25 scudi for the picture, a good sum of money for the time. But although Titian admired the animals he could not resist retouching the sky and landscape. This tremulous touch is to be recognized in the background, which recalls those of such late Titians as *Venus and Cupid* in the Galleria Borghese, Rome, and *Nymph and Shepherd* in the Kunsthistorisches Museum, Vienna. Titian also painted the eagle on the gangplank, a deferential reference to the House of Habsburg, and reworked the horses and their groom on the extreme right. Although this first version is undoubtedly the creation of Jacopo Bassano, he and Titian are not the only ones to have worked on the canvas. W. R. Rearick[49] suggests that due to the large size of the work, 207 × 265cm (81 × 104in), Jacopo relied to a considerable extent on the assistance of his eldest son, Francesco, who laid in many of the preliminary broad areas of paint and brought some portions, including the animals, near to completion before Jacopo returned to revise, correct and complete the work.

Rearick further informs us that during the 1580s Jacopo was to rely more and more on the collaboration of his sons, and a number of works bear the joint signatures of Jacopo and Francesco. To meet the increasing demand for his popular genre-like pictures Jacopo had to set up a kind of picture factory to mass-produce them in series. His son Francesco was the first to be set to work, who was soon joined by Giambattista, then by Leandro (1557–1662) and much later by Gerolamo (1566–1621). Jacopo Bassano's designs were mass-produced by his sons and assistants well into the seventeenth century. Some of these pictures are known in as many as 30 versions, and the *Animals Entering the Ark* was one of the most popular.

It will be noticed that my fragment corresponds to some extent with the left-hand side of the Prado picture, but in reverse; a look through some of the variations shows that none of the versions of the *Animals Entering the Ark* is a faithful replica of another picture. They are all, for better or for worse, individual works of art. They vary in quality immensely, and whereas Jacopo's original picture is a masterpiece, some of the late versions are pitifully bad. In between are some handsome pictures of considerable decorative value, and such would seem to have been the work of which my fragment once formed half. After owning the fragment for some 30 years, I could not help but try to imagine what the whole picture had once looked like. Growing tired of living with only half a picture, I resolved to reconstruct the missing section.

This may very well have remained a resolve had not the BBC commissioned a film documentary about me in 1991 entitled *Portrait of a Master Faker*. It struck me that it would fascinate viewers to see an Old Master painting grow up from the blank, white canvas to the upper layers of glazes and varnish, complete with old cracks – especially if it could be compared with genuine work side by side. In the event this idea was not used in the film, but it did stimulate me to carry out my long standing project (*see* plates 43–8).

My first task was to reline the fragment and put it on to a canvas a little larger than the size of the final work to allow for stretching. The old painting had been relined sometime early in this century. To bring the surface of the new half up to the same level I was obliged to lay down two thicknesses of good-quality canvas.

As the work had to be completed within three weeks, there was no time for me to use the flake-white ground of the Old Masters mentioned in the previous chapter, as this requires at least a month before one can work on it safely. Nor did I want to add a siccative such as raw umber because it would have destroyed the pure whiteness that I needed to reflect light from within the picture. So I used a commercially prepared undercoat as used by house painters. From this it is clear that my intention was simply to satisfy the eye, not chemical analysis. Nevertheless, the method I was to employ was essentially that of Bassano as he had learnt it from Titian. At this point I can hear someone asking: 'How on earth do you know what Bassano's method was?' This reminds me of a story told of W. B. Yeats, who on giving a poetry reading was asked why he declaimed his verse in the manner he did. The poet answered that this was because it was Homer's way, which, of course, led him to being questioned as to how he knew it was Homer's way. Whereupon Yeats responded: 'The quality of the man warrants the assumption.' Similarly, I know how Bassano painted his pictures because the end-result speaks of the means.

The Underdrawing

The first thing to do was to make a drawing of the missing half of the picture directly on to the white canvas in charcoal. I started extending the gangplank and completing the outlines of the two lions on it. Then moving downward I drew the figure of Noah, of which only a tiny area of drapery on the right side of the picture gave a clue, and then completed the drawing of the peacock. For the major motifs on my recreated side of the picture I used the following sources.

The head of Noah (below left) is not taken directly from any particular painting. It is a type that occurs in numerous Bassano and Bassanoesque pictures. It resembles, for instance, two heads in the *The Descent of the Holy Spirit* in the Museo Civico, Bassano (one is shown below right).

The two boys with a horse (below) are based on figures in *Rest on the Flight into Egypt* in the Pinacoteca Ambrosiana, Milan (bottom). In the Milan picture the boys are with a donkey rather than a horse, and the light is coming from the opposite direction.

The ruined shepherd's hut in the background (top) is yet again a common motif in the work of the Bassanos, and my version is similar to the hut in the background of *Santissima Trinità*, a painting by Jacopo Bassano in the parish church of Angarano (above). The figure on the extreme left (*see* p. 130, left) is based on a figure (also placed on the extreme left) from the *Baptism of St Lucilla* in the Museo Civico, Bassano (*see* p. 130, right).

The connecting passages among these major elements are generally of my own invention. The fox who looks with longing on the poultry is my idea, as are the two harts whose heads and necks frame a shape that makes a pun

on the English word 'heart', thus telling the observant English-speaking viewer that the painter also speaks English.

Having completed the drawing in charcoal, I went over the outlines with a fine brush dipped in raw umber diluted with turpentine. When these lines had dried, the charcoal was brushed off and the shadows indicated with the raw umber mixture. What I had on the canvas was, in fact, a complete drawing in line and wash.

The Underpainting

Having worked out the design, the next stage was to complete the underpainting. This was carried out using flake white and raw umber with turpentine as the vehicle. The umber would make the paint mixture dry quickly and the use of only turpentine ensured that the important principle of 'fat over lean' would be respected. In actual fact it is most likely that Bassano would have used burnt sienna in place of the umber, as Titian did. But, as it will be explained below, my problem was to match the colouring of the original half as it has survived. The sienna might have provided too warm a base; one offering no contrast for the warm browns that were to be superimposed. In this underpainting I was careful not to use a full range of tone.

That is to work in the middle register and save my darkest and lightest tones for the final painting.

The Final Paint Layers

It was, of course, essential to make the colouring of my half match the colouring of the original half. The great extent to which the colouring of the old part of the picture had altered was clear from a comparison with paintings by Bassano that have survived in better condition. The great glory of Venetian painting in the days of Bassano was colour, and his colouring, when fresh, is magnificent. In my picture, however, all but the flake white and the earth colours had decayed. No doubt the peacock in the foreground was placed where it is to introduce a splendid streak of colour, but now I could match its one peacock blue with lamp black and its gorgeous rainbow of a tail with a dingy brown. What saves the picture from being a total wreck is the fact that Bassano loaded his lights and kept his shadows transparent. The flake white has not suffered any serious change of colour, and the darkening of the other colours has to some extent been compensated for by a certain inner glow coming from the ground and underpainting. Thus, at least, the whole tonal design is preserved.

To achieve a patina on the horse's head and other areas of white, I waited until the paint was quite dry and sandpapered it down slightly before applying a glaze with a little burnt umber and gold yellow, into which I would paint again with thickish paint. This process was repeated two or three times. The colours used were very few: flake white, yellow ochre, Venetian red (a form of red ochre), the umbers and lamp black, all from our forger's palette. Incidentally, I made a point of not touching the original half of the picture at all. This remains exactly as I bought it, without the slightest intercession on my part. So should any future owner prefer to live with only the original fragment and sit there wondering what was on the missing half they may easily remove my contribution, or, if they have the talent, replace it with their own reconstruction.

As for the cracks and other signs of age necessary to bring my half of the design into harmony with the original, that is a subject to be dealt with in the next chapter, where the reader will find a number of 'ageing' techniques described. Before turning to them, some mention must be made of the most common form of faking Old Master paintings: modifying old pictures to suit a modern market.

In an article published in *Hemisphere* (July 1994), Frederich W. Waterman tells this story:

> Less talented forgers occasionally take old paintings and, in an effort to make these works more bankable, try to adapt the subject or scene. A common ruse is to 'find' the ancestor of an illustrious family and offer the painting to a wealthy descendant. Of course this backfires pretty badly if the forger doesn't know art history.
>
> Alfred Du Pont, former head of the Du Pont company, was approached by a Philadelphia dealer claiming to have a portrait of Du Pont's great-great grandmother holding her infant son. The asking price was $25,000. When Du Pont refused, noticing two artistic styles in the portrait, the dealer dropped the price to $10,000, then $1,000 and, in desperation $400, which Du Pont accepted, believing the frame to be worth that much. A curator at the Philadelphia Museum examined the painting and found that the eighteenth-century clothing had been painted over the subject's original seventeenth-century apparel. After removing the new paint, the curator discovered that the original work was by Murillo. The $400 painting was reassessed at $150,000.

This does seem to indicate a rather naive forger and a shrewd buyer. Let us, for fun, rewrite the scenario: millionaire X is known to be a nervous buyer who will only acquire a picture if he is certain of getting a bargain. To this end he always has any picture offered to him vetted by Y, the curator of a local museum. One day he is approached by Z, a New York dealer, with a picture purporting to be of X's great-great grand uncle. The painting is still wet, and this awakens X's rarely dormant suspicions. While dealer Z's back is turned, he surreptitiously wipes away a little of the fresh paint to reveal a small area of what seems to be an old picture underneath. 'May I hold on to the picture for a few days?' asks X. 'I'm sure I will grow to love it, as will Mrs X.' The dealer agrees, and as soon as he has left, X is on the phone explaining to Y that he may have made a very exciting find. The curator examines the picture, and his expert opinion confirms that the paint is wet, adding that this is a most unusual feature of eighteenth-century portraits. Perhaps it might be worth having an X-ray photograph taken.

To the satisfaction of both collector and curator, the X-ray reveals what appears to be a portrait by van Dyck lurking behind the millionaire's great-great grand uncle. At which Mr X cannot wait to pay dealer Z his asking price of $25,000 and so become the proud owner of a $250,000 picture. Meanwhile, back at the studio, a gleeful Vincent van Blank paints yet another Old Master picture on which to paint some wealthy person's ancestor. I am not suggesting for a moment that Mr Du Pont was duped, at $400 he was safe enough, but I would warn even the shrewdest buyer to beware. A little connoisseurship is a dangerous thing.

There are innumerable examples of paintings being doctored to make them more saleable. Writing in my autobiography of my own apprenticeship during the fifties in that form of alchemy that can turn a painting into gold, I said:

> Pictures that are unsaleable are bad business and by some warped kind of logic become bad art. Nobody wants bad art, so dealers have it improved ... should a painting be unsaleable because it represented an ugly woman, the ugly woman would become a pretty young girl. If it represented a saleable young man contemplating an unsaleable skull, the offending skull was changed into a brimming glass of wine or some other object with commercially viable associations. A cat added to the foreground guaranteed the sale of the dullest landscape. Dogs and horses enlivened otherwise unsaleable pastures. Balloons floated into commercially deficient skies at once becoming immensely important (that is, expensive) documents in the history of aviation. Popular signatures came, and unpopular signatures went. Sullen-faced individuals left our easels wreathed in smiles. Poppies bloomed in dull-coloured fields. Unknown sitters transformed themselves into illustrious statesmen, generals, admirals, actors, actresses, musicians and men of letters. So, like librettist W. S. Gilbert's king, whose heart was twice as good as gold, we ... to the top of every tree promoted everybody.[50]

No doubt such businesses as that of the restorer, for whom I was working, still thrive and may be considered as universities for forgers.

CHAPTER TEN

More Wrinkles

'It is in the ability to deceive oneself that the greatest talent

is shown.'

ANATOLE FRANCE

Just like old paper, old panels and canvases need no ageing. Earth colours that may have lain in the ground for millions of years clearly need no attention from us on behalf of time; what was said in Chapter 5 about ageing drawings is equally applicable to paintings: age gracefully. If the picture you have made has any artistic merit at all it deserves to be treated with respect. Why reduce it to a worthless wreck? Then, again, we have this foolish habit, common to the majority of art forgers, to paint with no regard to the picture's supposed age other than following an old model. That is to say that their 'antique' paintings are literally as fresh as new paint, and it is not until they have completed them that they make a belated attempt to age them. The work of the master faker, on the other hand, has every appearance of age from its mellow start. His or her ground either is, or at least looks as if it is, of the time of the artist that they are following; their underdrawing, too, has the appearance of being old, as does their underpainting. In consequence, when they have completed the final layer, the picture already has a sense, or an atmosphere, of true age. After all, the lower layers affect the upper layers in such a way that one might say the picture has had age built into it.

Ageing Old Panels
If you have not been able to procure a period panel, then you must find the oldest wood available. Even for a decorative painting, plywood and such stuff

is anti-aesthetic, so at least have sufficient respect for your work to get a real piece of timber. This acquired, you may make worm-holes and darken the wood to match the age required. Nevertheless, there is no way that these things can be artificially achieved well enough to deceive the connoisseur.

Imitation worm-holes

One of the ways of imitating worm-holes, once much used by makers of 'antique' furniture, is to fire lead shot at the piece of wood under treatment. This has at least two disadvantages: first, the holes made are at right angles to the surface, rather than turning to burrow into the wood to make tunnels parallel with the surface, as with real worm-holes; second, one has to remove the lead shot. Drilling is an alternative, but the holes produced also run at right angles to the surface. Beating the surface with a very coarse file until it has a very worm-eaten look is yet another method, and readers may invent their own. But best of all is the worm itself, for in this case only the worm will turn.

Darkening wood

Most timber grows darker with age, and panels over 300 years old may be so dark as to be almost black. Obviously the various tints can be matched by any number of stains. Even colours from our own forger's palette such as the umbers, black and burnt sienna, in judicious mixtures and well diluted with turpentine, will do. What we cannot so easily imitate is the satin-like patina of old wood. One can get close to it with the cunning use of tinted waxes, but the result is never quite good enough to fool the experienced eye.

Ageing New Canvas

New canvas, which for our work should always be linen of the finest quality, can be distinguished from canvas made before the late eighteenth century by the fact that it is machine-made. This gives to it a more regular texture. As a rule this cannot be detected through the various paint layers of the finished picture, and the art sleuth will examine the back of the painting for any evidence of failure on our part to have found a genuinely old support. The simplest course we can take to thwart them in their investigation is to have our picture relined. There are specialists who will do this for us, but we can quite easily do it ourselves.

How to reline a painting

Materials

1. A perfectly even, flat surface.
2. A thermostatically controlled iron.
3. A piece of felt slightly larger than the picture.
4. Equal parts of pure beeswax and mastic varnish.
5. A round hog's-hair brush, not less than 2.5cm (1in) across.
6. A new piece of canvas, sufficiently larger than the painting to allow for the relined picture to be put on a stretcher.

Method

1. Lay the felt on the table with the picture face down upon it.
2. Heat the wax and mastic varnish together in a double boiler, and stir until thoroughly mixed.
3. Give both the back of your painting and one side of the new canvas a generous coat of the wax–resin mixture.
4. Unite the two canvases, using an iron that is just hot enough to melt the mixture sandwiched between them. The iron is passed over the back of the new support rapidly and systematically, and always from the centre.

The purpose of the felt is to protect the impasto (always supposing that you want to protect it) from being flattened against the unyielding surface of the table or whatever we may be working on. The traditional way of protecting a painting during the relining process is to reinforce it with layers of tissue-paper applied with a water-soluble adhesive. If a piece of felt is difficult to obtain this method may well be used. One may also use adhesives other than the wax–resin mixture recommended above. I have found myself successfully using Polycell, and doubtless there are many other patent brands of adhesives that might be employed, but they must have a certain amount of flexibility. Nevertheless, a wax–resin mixture has a number of advantages. Not least among them, from our point of view, is that it consolidates the painting by impregnation through both the canvas and the cracks from the back to the front. Exactly how useful this can be for us will be explained below under size cracking.

Relining not only conceals our modern canvas but also makes our production more credible because by far the greatest number of genuine Old Master paintings of any importance have, in fact, undergone exactly the same treatment. Moreover, if we should have carried out our relining less than perfectly, we will have a nicely flattened impasto and a tonality introduced that we didn't really intend, which, like all good restorers, we can blame on the incompetence of some former one.

If, for some reason, relining is out of the question, the best thing to do is to reduce the thickness of the new canvas by wearing it away with a sanding machine. Be careful to do this in such a way as to leave no sign of the operation in the form of lines showing in which direction the machine has been moved. To do this requires using the sander in every direction, with a predominance of a rotary motion, and completing the operation with the finest sandpaper available. Carried out well, this sandpapering will leave the canvas so consumed that the investigator, looking for little knots and irregularities of handwoven canvas, will find that time has worn them all away, and there is nothing to be done but have the painting transferred to a stronger support. In which case the buyer will do the relining for you.

How to stain a canvas
Having worn down your new canvas, you will need to stain it. This is partly because canvases are, in one respect, like panels: they darken with age. And also because there are reasons quite other than sandpapering to account for the fragility of truly old canvas, and these natural causes leave signs. One common cause for the deterioration of old canvas is damp. Humidity attacks the unprotected backs of old paintings, and it is this fact that makes it credible that your time-consumed canvas is affected on one side only. Damp leaves stains, and these you may produce either naturally by leaving your canvas in a dank cellar or some other place of the kind that mushrooms find congenial, or cosmetically with your forger's palette, just as you would for panels. If you are to do this expertly, you must base your work on a study of genuinely old paintings. So back to the saleroom, where you will notice that it is often the case, where damp has attacked a painting, that one edge has been damaged more seriously than the others. Usually it is the bottom edge, suggesting that the painting was once badly stored, and was left in contact with a damp floor.

If in the course of reducing your canvas (not your painting) to a pitiful condition you have inadvertently broken through to cause a small hole or two, these must be neatly repaired, as must any tears or weakening of the canvas around the edges that might make the stretching of the canvas impossible. These repairs are made with patches and strip lining.

How to patch holes

1. Lay the picture face down on plate-glass, with the damaged area in contact with greased paper.
2. Cut a piece of unprimed canvas – of the same weight or slightly lighter weight than the one used for the actual picture – to the right size for generously covering the hole.
3 Pull out several threads from the weave all round in order to thin the edges. This will prevent the shape of the patch appearing on the face of the picture.
4. Paper the wax–resin adhesive in the manner described above when speaking of relining, and use it to put the patch in place, pressing with a hot iron.
5. Turn the picture over, remove the greased paper and stop the hole with the kind of putty that house painters use to fill holes in woodwork before painting. This can be bought at any hardware store, or you can make it yourself by mixing whiting together with linseed oil. Now it only remains to retouch the area with colour, and you have added yet another touch of authenticity to your creation.

How to reinforce the edges of a canvas
This operation is carried out exactly as for patching. The strips are cut long enough to cover the circumference of the canvas and broad enough to extend from the outside edges to the inside edges of the stretcher. The inside edges should not, however, extend beyond the width of the stretcher. The strip-lined canvas must be put in a press or kept under weights for at least 24 hours.

The Effects of Time
The major effects of time on old paintings are two: a lowering of tone and cracking of the paint.

Lowering of tone in oil paintings
The most common cause for the lowering of tone in an old painting is the darkening of the oil. This was known by the Old Masters themselves. In a

letter to his friend the French scholar Nicholas Claude de Peiresc, dated London, 9th August 1629, Rubens wrote:

> If I knew that my portrait was still in Antwerp, I would ask them to hold it and open the box to see whether it had been damaged or if it had darkened. This often happens to fresh colours when they have been packed away in a box and have not been exposed to light and air. Should my picture not look as well as when it was finished, the best remedy would be to put it in the sun, and the excess oil that causes such change will be destroyed. Should it darken again after a while, repeat this process, which is the only remedy.

Naturally the Old Masters were not all that keen on having their pictures darken (quite quickly, from Rubens' account) and did everything they could to prevent it. This mostly consisted of purifying and bleaching their oils. Exposure to the sun and air is both the oldest and best means of clarifying. Other methods include washing, filtering and the adding of bleaching agents such as hydrogen peroxide or pure grain alcohol, but none of these procedures is permanently successful, and the oil will sooner or later revert to its natural tendency to darken. All this, of course, is something that does not trouble the forger in the least. Quite the opposite: the lowering of the tone of the oil does not take place nearly fast enough to our purposes, and we are obliged to have recourse to artificial means of obtaining the effect.

One might imagine that the simplest method of doing this might be to darken the oil before use, but this, curiously, is not the case. One can, in fact, paint with a very dark oil indeed, and yet it will not materially alter the appearance of the colour – unless the oil is so greatly in excess of what is needed to prepare the pigment that the resulting paint has not enough body for practical use.

An example of exactly how dark an oil can be used and not affect the tone of a paint of normal consistency is furnished by the popularity, earlier in this century, of a painting medium invented by Jacques Maroger (1884–1962) and named after him. Maroger was a French picture restorer and one time head of restoration at the Louvre in Paris. An English translation of his theories was published in 1948 under the title *The Secret Formulas and Techniques of the Masters*. Although his views are not supported by modern authorities, many artists, including myself, have experimented with the Maroger medium, which contains two parts that are mixed together at the time of painting. One is a 'black' oil, which is produced by boiling either linseed or nut oil together with litharge (a form of lead monoxide) or flake white which, being a carbonate of lead, gives similar results. This dangerous operation is carried out in a double-boiler and the greatest care taken that not a drop of water enters the liquid as it can explode. The second ingredient is mastic varnish. The resulting Maroger medium is a jelly, with which it is pleasant enough to paint but that would seem to have little to do with the Old Masters. The only reason I bring it up here is because, although the oil is literally black, it has no noticeable effect on the tone of the colours; even the whites and blues remain virtually unaffected.

From what has been said it will be understood that simply darkening the oil we use is not going to darken our paintings. The solution to our problem is simplicity itself: we merely paint our oil pictures the tone we wish them to have, that is rich and low. This we do by lowering the tone of our highlight with one of the umbers. Raw umber is usually the better one to use because it preserves a coolness in the colours, which is a good antidote to the too hot effect that can sometimes come about by the tinted varnishes that we shall be speaking of below.

This method is perfectly acceptable from the chemical point of view, because the Old Masters themselves frequently mixed the umbers with flake white and other colours, either to modify the tone or to hasten the drying. This last point is very important to us because it is necessary that we give our pictures every chance of drying through as rapidly as is consonant with allowing us time to paint without haste.

Lowering of tone in tempera paintings
Paintings in egg tempera are much less susceptible to lowering in tone than oil paintings, and many examples from the fourteenth century onward are in this respect as fresh as when they were painted. What lowering of tone there may be is largely due to surface dirt. This dirt, which often includes candle smoke, has mostly been in contact with the painted surface for so many years that it has become virtually part of the final layer of paint. This is why too zealous a cleaning to remove all traces of dirt must perforce remove some of the painted surface itself. To make our slight film of dirt adhere to, or, more correctly, bind with, the painting we must create a delicate tooth on to which it may hold, and, similarly, as we did when preparing our panel to hold the gesso, we must very slightly roughen our surface to hold the dirt. Some of this roughness will be supplied by the

cracks, but in between the cracks we will need some texture. This fine texture must in no way look regular or mechanical. Remember that in old pictures it is the natural wear and tear of centuries – a knock here, a scratch there, a rub, a polish, a too-vigorous dusting or slight scrubbing – but not all on one and the same day. So you must use your judgement in the handling of your abrasives, whether these be sandpaper, pumice powder or whatever, and never miss the happy accident. A story is told about the Italian faker Ioni, famous for his Italian 'primitives', who was studying one of his panels on the roof of his medieval tower in Siena when, as he was wondering what might happen to it were it to fall from that height to the ground, the panel really did slip through his fingers. On retrieving the picture the artist was delighted to find a most convincing split right through the centre, which he happily restored to perfection.

Having skilfully roughened the texture of our tempera painting we may apply our dirt, which, if we wish to deceive the scientist, must be just that. Han van Meegeren made the mistake of filling his cracks with ink, but the contents of the vacuum cleaner, dust from the street or good old-fashioned dirt, combined with an evaporating spirit such as rectified petrol, is much better. And don't forget a little candle smoke and the tiniest touch of wax.

Cracking

CAUSES OF CRACKING IN OLD PAINTINGS

Egg tempera and oil have proved themselves with time to be satisfactory binding media, giving to pigments the stability upon which their life depends. Nevertheless, they both in differing degrees suffer from a tendency to shrink and become brittle with age. A picture that has survived even 100 years will normally be covered with a fine network of micro-cracks, which, because they hold dust and other foreign matter, show up as dark lines where they cross the light areas of the painting. This pattern of micro-cracks that develops across the surface of old paintings we call 'craquelure'. The causes of craquelure may be many, but the major factor involved is a loss of elasticity in the brittle old medium, which forbids the necessary flexibility to adjust to the movements of the support as it alternately shrinks and expands in response to changes of humidity in the atmosphere. Craquelure should not be confused with cracks or cleavages running inwards at right angles to the surface that may very well penetrate through all layers of paint, including the ground.

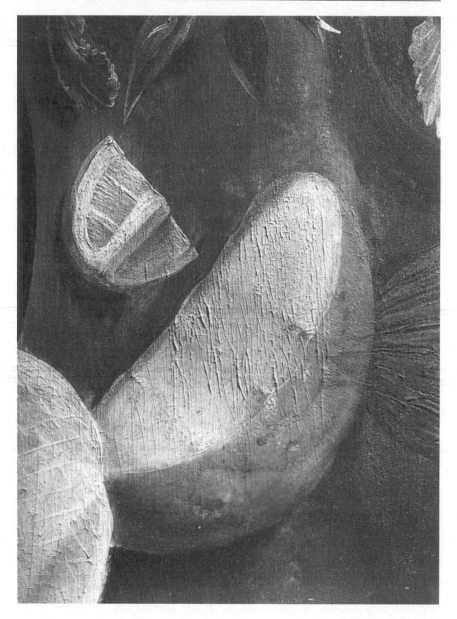

Differences in craquelure caused by the various drying rates of the pigments used (detail is shown sideways)

Opposite: Chalk or gresso grounds create porcelain-like cracks that follow the grain of the wood on a wooden panel

Plate 28 Draughtsmanship, although unfashionable these days, is a useful attribute. Extensive and complete preparatory work will save endless wasted hours later on.

Jan van Eyck (active 1422–41), *St Barbara*, preparatory drawing on panel, Museum voor Schone Kunsten/Musée des Beaux-Arts, Antwerp.

Copies are not necessarily inferior to the originals. Turner was so proud of his version of one of Claude's great masterpieces that he left it to the English Nation on condition that it should be hung in the National Gallery next to the Claude original.

Plate 29 J.M.W. Turner (1775–1851), *Dido Building Carthage*, oil on canvas, National Gallery, London.

Plate 30 Claude Lorrain (1604/5–82), *Seaport with the Embarkation of the Queen of Sheba*, oil on canvas, National Gallery, London.

Curiously, but perhaps not surprisingly, a copy by a famous name will cost more than the original work by another artist who is less well known. In 1976, a sale at Christie's proved this point beyond doubt, even though van de Velde was hardly a minor name, and of whom Turner himself was in awe.

Plate 31 Willem van de Velde the Younger (1633–1707), *Approaching Storm*, oil on canvas, sold at Christie's, London in 1976 for £65,000.

Plate 32 J.M.W. Turner (1775–1851), *Approaching Storm*, in the manner of Willem van de Velde the Younger (1633–1707), oil on canvas, sold at Christie's, London in 1976 for £340,000.

Plate 33 On old canvas with an appropriate inscription added to the reverse, could this copy have passed as a version of Turner's famous painting by William Etty, a great nineteenth-century artist known to have been influenced by Turner?

Eric Hebborn, *The Fighting Téméraire*, after J.M.W. Turner (1775–1851), oil on canvas, Estate of Eric Hebborn, Rome.

Plate 34 J.M.W. Turner (1775–1851), *The Fighting Téméraire*, oil on canvas, National Gallery, London.

Of the two drawings illustrated in plates 35 and 36, although the original design was Flaxman's own, the Goya would fetch many times more on the open market. Despite the balance of advice favouring modesty, it occasionally pays to think big. After all, it takes as much work to sell a Rolls-Royce as it does a bicycle.

Plate 35 John Flaxman (1755–1826), *Hypocrits*, illustration for canto XXIII of Dante, *Inferno*, published in 1807.

Plate 36 Francisco de Goya (1747–1828) reworked Flaxman's design for *Three Pairs of Hooded Figures*, indian ink on buff-coloured laid paper, Biblioteca Nacional, Madrid.

Despite the greatness of his own work, Delacroix's copies of Rubens and Raphael number somewhere in the region of a hundred. His motives for such arduous reverence were purely educational, a sentiment which cannot be recommended strongly enough.

Plate 37 Peter Paul Rubens (1577–1640), central panel of *The Descent from the Cross*, oil on panel, Kathedraal van Onze-Lieve-Vrouw, Antwerp.

Plate 38 Eugène Delacroix (1798–1863), *Sketch for Descent from the Cross*, after Peter Paul Rubens (1577–1640), pen and brown ink on paper, Museum Boymans-van Beuningen, Rotterdam.

Plate 39 A decorative fake in red, black and white chalk over a photographic reproduction of the original drawing which was bought at the Uffizi, Florence.
  Eric Hebborn, *Portrait of a Young Boy Wearing a Cap and Other Studies*, after Il Pontormo (1594–1657), red, black and white chalk over photographic reproduction, private collection, London.

Plate 40 A pastiche of unknown origin copying from unrelated pictures, attempting to be a rare double portrait of the fifteenth century. The sources have been identified as plates 41 and 42, Botticelli and Pollaiuolo.

Plate 41 Sandro Botticelli (1445–1510), *Portrait of a Woman (La Bella Simonetta)*, oil on panel, Palazzo Pitti, Florence.

Plate 42 Attributed to Piero del Pollaiuolo (*c*.1443–96), *Profile of a Woman*, tempera and oil on panel, Museo Poldi-Pezzoli, Milan.

In the early 1960s, Hebborn acquired a fragment of a studio painting by the Bassanos, and decided to complete the missing part thirty years later, based on a completed painting in the Prado, Madrid (plate 49). The sequence of photographs (plates 43–8) shows the work in progress.

Plate 43 Right half: studio of Jacopo and Francesco Bassano (*c.*1535–92), *The Animals Entering the Ark*, fragment, oil on canvas; left half: primed canvas.

Plate 44 Sized canvas.

Plate 45
Under-drawing.

Plate 46 The first painted sections.

Plate 47 The picture almost completed.

Plate 48 The completed painting *The Animals Entering the Ark*, original fragment by studio of Jacopo and Francesco Bassano (*c.*1535–92) (right half), completed by Eric Hebborn (left half), oil on canvas, Estate of Eric Hebborn, Rome.

Plate 49 Jacopo and Francesco Bassano (*c.*1535–92), *The Animals Entering the Ark*, oil on canvas, Museo del Prado, Madrid.

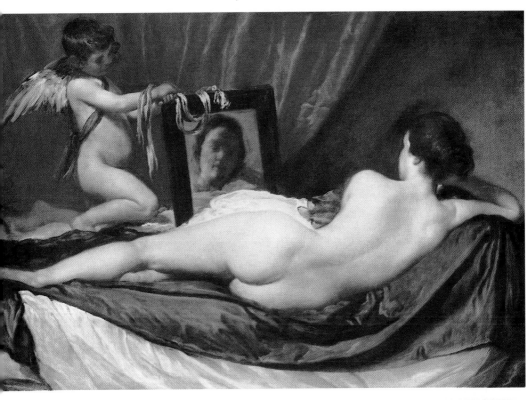

Painters who do not smooth
out their brushwork are
signing their work with
every stroke. Details of
paintings (plates 50–3) have
been enlarged to allow the
reader to compare the brushwork of some of the greatest
Old Masters.

Plate 50 Diego Velasquez
(1599–1660), *Toilet of Venus*,
oil on canvas, National
Gallery, London.

Plate 51 An analysis of the brushwork of this painting formerly attributed to Rembrandt suggests to the author that the demotion of the painting may have been poorly judged.

Follower of Rembrandt Harmensz. van Rijn (1606–69), *A Man in a Room*, formerly known as *A Philosopher in his Study*, oil on panel, National Gallery, London.

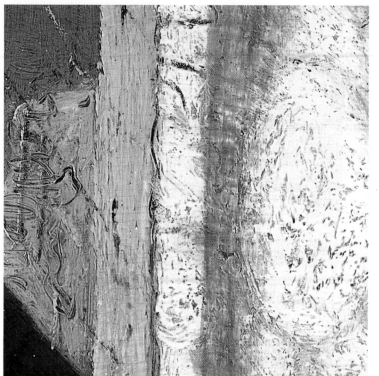

Plate 52 *opposite* Rembrandt Harmensz. van Rijn (1606–69), *Self-Portrait Aged Sixty-three*, oil on canvas, National Gallery, London.

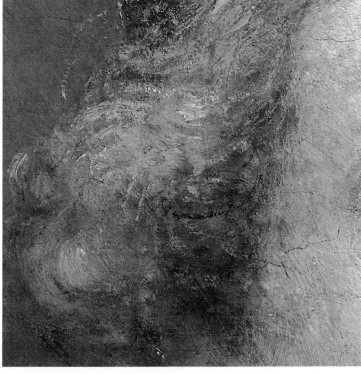

Plate 53 Frans Hals (1580–1666), *Young Man Holding a Skull*, oil on canvas, National Gallery, London.

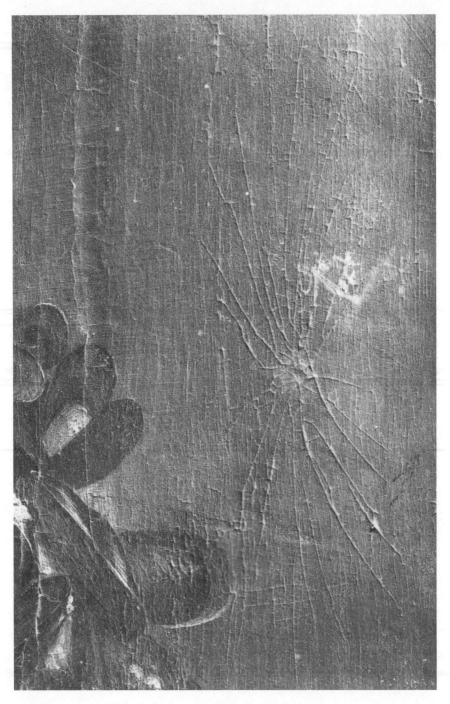

A picture that has survived even 100 years will normally be covered with an agreeable network of varied craquelure

Opposite: Cracks caused by local tension (detail is shown sideways)

Other reasons for cracking, given by Hilaire Hiler,[51] are:

1. Resinous varnishes and vehicles mixed unevenly with colours, causing different rates of drying.
2. The application of coats of paint before the underlying coat is thoroughly dry and with no consideration of the differing drying rates.
3. The presence of bitumen.
4. The presence of glue chalk or gesso grounds, which may be responsible for porcelain-like cracks that usually follow the grain of wood on a wooden panel. These cracks are so fine that they tend to do the picture little harm.
5. The presence of grounds that are too smooth, fine or non-absorbent. The paint may 'crawl' or 'creep', creating fine but disagreeable cracks, which form concave saucer-like depressions.
6. The tendency for varnish to crack, usually in polygonal patterns, which is at its worst on the darkest portions of the picture.
7. A picture that was varnished before it was thoroughly dry.
8. Due to the movement of the support in absorbing and giving up humidity, cracks can occur on very old pictures on canvas. They are regular and fine, with the edges slightly curled up. Oxidization and brittleness of the old canvas, which has lost all elasticity and life, is another reason for cracking.
9. A too-absorbent ground that has taken up too much of the binder, particularly in the case of certain pigments such as the ochres and raw sienna. This can cause irregular cracks, which do not get much worse with time and usually take place within six months of the picture's completion, that may be repaired with retouching varnish in the studio.
10. A framework that is not bevelled deeply enough. In this case physical shocks and jars may cause the canvas to crack round the edges.
11. By putting thin paint over fat, a condition that is similar to a too-smooth and non-absorbent ground.

The common factor in all but number ten of the above, which depends on physical shock, is the inability of one layer of paint, varnish, ground or support to maintain its rapport in regard to its upstairs or downstairs neighbour. Knowing this, we learn how to put our pictorial layers in friendly conflict with each other to produce cracks that, like a wise man's wrinkles, enhance rather than disfigure. If Time has not drawn them himself with his 'antique pen' we are merely anticipating his handiwork. But before speaking of how to create cracks we must first address the problem of how to preserve them.

HOW TO PRESERVE CRACKS IN OLD GROUNDS

When we have been fortunate enough to find an old picture to strip to its ground we will find that this foundation is covered with cracks. The connoisseur will tell you that the forger gives himself away when using old grounds because his new paint fills in the old cracks – something that can often be seen with the naked eye and, in any case, is as plain as can be with the slightest magnification. To avoid being unmasked in this elementary matter is not as difficult as it might at first appear, and here is a very simple method developed from certain etching techniques.

An etching plate ready for printing, in so far as it is covered with incised lines, resembles our old painting ground. The etcher has to fill these lines with ink, yet leave the surface of his plate free of ink to print white. To do this nowadays he uses a flexible plastic spatula that forces the ink into the lines while wiping it off the surface, which then only requires a final wipe with a rag to be perfectly clean. Now what we have to do is to fill up the old cracks on our ground with a substance that, when the picture is completed, we may remove to leave the painting with fissures running down from the surface to the support. The method of filling the cracks is, of course, exactly that for filling the lines of an etching plate with ink. But what of the substance?

A TEMPORARY FILLING FOR CRACKS WHILE PAINTING

There is another etching technique that has always caught my imagination, and it is known as aquatint. The reason for its fascination in my eyes stems from the fact that I can't imagine how it works. Let me very briefly describe it. Instead of being engraved or etched into metal, the drawing is made directly on to the metal plate with a black gouache dissolved in sugar-water. The whole plate is then covered with a wax ground. Now this wax ground is what protects those parts of the plate from the acid that the etcher uses to incise his lines. Consequently, if the whole plate is covered with wax no part of it should be prone to being bitten by the acid. Contrary to what should be the case, when the plate with the sugar-gouache drawing is immersed into the acid bath it is not long before bubbles begin to appear over the drawn areas, showing that the wax has given way, and the acid is biting the design into the metal.

This process is essentially what we are going to do with our old cracks. We are going to fill them first with a substance containing sugar, then cover them with our waterproof paint (which takes the part of the wax) and finally soak the surface of our painting with water (which corresponds to the acid) to remove the new paint covering the cracks. This will leave our water-soluble filler exposed, to be easily removed from our genuinely old cracks that have now come right through to the surface. The mixture I use for this temporary filler is a water-soluble size, usually employed for hanging wallpaper and sold in powder form. To three tablespoons of this size or paste I add one teaspoon of sugar. The ingredients are mixed together with only just enough cold water to make a workable filler. This allows for the dryish mixture to interexpand and force itself out of the cracks. When (after the painting is finished) we gently sponge it over with hot water, piece by piece, the old cracks from the ground are revealed. Naturally the thicker the layer of paint covering the cracks the less likely the paint is to give way, but the effect of certain cracks going up to but not across areas of thick paint is not uncommon in genuinely old works.

THE USE OF SIZE IN CRACKING
Size is one of the most useful cracking agents at our disposal. This is largely because its effects are relatively easy to control. With its help we can, if we wish, start a cracking process that will in a short time (anything from two weeks to two years) crack a painting right through from the ground to the surface. All we have to do is to size our raw canvas rather more strongly than usual and then dry the size very rapidly in the sun or in front of a fire. Anything painted on top of this now brittle size will easily crack and have a tendency to flake and fall off. Naturally this paint loss is not desirable in too great a quantity and once cracks begin to appear in satisfactory numbers the process may be checked by impregnating the canvas from the back with wax or a wax–resin mixture.

Size may also be used to crack paint and varnish by brushing it on top of them and again drying the glue rapidly. The stronger the size and the more rapid the drying, the more damage it will do.

Another use for size is to put a coat of it over the finished painting before the final varnish. This is to thwart what is known as the alcohol test. New paint is much more easily dissolved in alcohol than old paint, and some art sleuth is quite likely to test your picture by pecking at a corner of it with a wad of cotton-wool soaked in the solvent. If, however, you have taken the precaution to coat your paint with size it will resist the alcohol.

CRACKING BY FRACTURE

A time-honoured method for cracking pictures is to roll them, paint inward, around a pole such as a broom handle. Unless your paint is very elastic it will fracture, producing cracks running parallel to the pole. You then roll your canvas up in the other direction to make cracks going at right angles to the first series, and then again diagonally until you have a nice network. A variant of this method is to rub the painting over the edge of a table.

CRACKING BY BAKING

There is a popular myth that forgers bake their Old Masters to produce cracks. It is true that rapid changes of temperature can induce cracks, but the principal reason why some fakes have been baked is to harden the paint, not to crack it. New paint is soft and remains relatively soft for decades. If, however, the paint has been mixed with a synthetic resin, such as the phenol-formaldehyde used by Han van Meegeren, and baked at a steady heat of 100–105°C (210–220°F) for two to three hours, the surface becomes very hard. It is very important if one is going to bake a painting that it be thoroughly dry. At least a year from making to baking should pass, otherwise the paint may bubble up as the oil simmers. The canvas should be taken off its stretcher and put in the centre of the oven where the hot air can circulate around it. If there are any very strong fumes coming off the picture, either the temperature is too high or the painting has not been sufficiently dried out. Tom Keating once said that he had never even baked so much as a cake, and indeed there is seldom a need for it.

If you have used your umbers freely to lower your picture's tone they will also have acted as dryers, and if the media and vehicles that you have employed are not too rich in oil, and contain a little hard resin-like copal in the final layer, after a year or so the paint should be hard enough to resist the thumbnail test for fresh paint. Or if a dent can still be made by the art sleuth's nail it will merely be assumed that the painting has been revarnished.

DRAWN CRACKS

For decorative fakes cracks can, with skill, be nicely imitated by drawing them on to or into the picture. Drawing them into the picture is done when the final layer of paint is still wet. This is carried out with a fine point such as those of pins or needles or fine nails; a fine pen can also be used. This method is most effective in the thinly painted areas and especially when the final layer of paint happens to be lighter than the colour beneath it. In the thicker areas of paint the instrument used will throw up a ridge on either side of the furrow it makes, which can easily be recognized for what it is under even slight magnification. In some cases these ridges can be removed by sandpapering when the paint has dried. Cracks drawn on to the painted surface are made with the very finest of sable brushes and with the use of a magnifying glass. Care is taken not to make them too dark and obvious.

Whether or not the cracks are drawn on to or into the painting they must follow the patterns of natural cracking, and it is a good idea to take real cracks as models, copying them from period pictures. It must always be borne in mind that the variety of patterns made by cracks is limitless, and many kinds may exist in one and the same picture. It is quite impossible to judge the age of a picture by the way it has cracked alone.

CRACKS CREATED BY VARNISH

It is rare that the artist's colourmen ever offer materials especially designed for the forger's use, but one firm at least does seem to have our interests at heart. Curiously enough, it is a French company. I say curiously because France is one of the countries where the forger has a particularly bad name and is, as a rule, treated pretty shabbily. The friendly firm is called Lefranc et Bourgeois, and they offer two picture varnishes intended to simulate age: the *Vernis à vieillir* (varnish for giving an appearance of age) (ref. 2313) and the *Vernis craqueleur* (crackle varnish) (ref. 2314).

Vernis à vieillir is extremely dark and gives the picture a golden glow. This is applied first and left to dry for a few hours until it is still fresh but not tacky. Then the *Vernis craqueleur* is applied on top of it, and, after a period of 20 minutes or so, cracks begin to appear. These cracks are then filled with a patina, also sold by Lefranc, so that they can be seen more easily. Instructions are given on the bottles, and the firm recommends either another coat of *Vernis à vieillir* or a wax varnish, depending on whether you want a glossy or matt finish. The matt-wax finish is, in my opinion, preferable, as it is not quite as obviously new and glossy.

One might imagine that so dark a varnish as *Vernis à vieillir* would radically alter one's colour scheme, but, in fact, it simply seems to unify it a little. A varnish has to be extraordinarily dark before it appreciably alters the colour of the picture.

This matter was the subject of an article in the *Burlington Magazine* (June 1962). The author of the article, J. Coburn Witherop, clearly agrees with me about the benefit to be derived by the scholar from practical experiment and proposes the following demonstration. Four varnishes are prepared:

1. A dark, hard copal resin-oil varnish, prepared by crushing the resin and heating for a long period with linseed oil.
2. A mastic resin-oil varnish prepared in the same way.
3. Dammer resin dissolved cold in rectified white spirit (mineral spirit).
4. A modern synthetic resin, AW2, dissolved cold in rectified white spirit (mineral spirit).

The colour of these varnishes as viewed in glass bottles may be described thus:

1. Very dark, reddish brown, semi-translucent.
2. Deep reddish gold, translucent.
3. Yellow with slightly milky sheen, transparent.
4. Almost water clear.

If we apply the four varnishes in separate, vertical strips over a freshly cleaned landscape, so that each covers an area of the painting – blue sky and white clouds, blue distance, green middle distance and the richly glazed and brown foreground – we will find that there is no appreciable difference between even the darkest and the palest of these varnishes. The difference will only become apparent with the passing of time, and with age it will increase. For a varnish to exert a definite colour effect it must be so stained or pigmented that it appears when seen in a bottle or jar to be paint and not varnish at all.

There is something about a glistening, newly cleaned picture, fresh from the restorer that makes one wonder how much repainting has been indulged in; even if one does not go so far as to think that the work is entirely new, one invariably wonders if the work is entirely old. Such doubts once raised may never be dispersed. This being so, your painting stands a better chance of making its way in the world if it has a matt varnish with a certain amount of surface dirt upon it. A recent writer recommends, for the adding of two centuries of dirt, 'Reverse the vacuum cleaner full force.' This method might coat the back of the canvas with a layer of dust, because it would have the texture of the canvas to hold it, but on the front the two centuries of dust would fall to the floor, and you would need to turn your vacuum cleaner back to its normal duties. A better method is to shake some dirt and dust together with a little dark pigment or stain with essence of petrol, and rub the mixture lightly over the thoroughly dried varnish. This will not only enrich the patina of the painting but also further reduce any unwanted shine.

Old Frames

Period frames are always an asset, especially if they have labels and inscriptions on the back to suggest a suitable provenance. Here again you must do your homework. For instance, there may be a lot number chalked on the back of the frame that an auction house could look up in an old sale catalogue. If your picture fits the description in the catalogue all well and good, but if you have painted, say, a marine subject and the catalogue describes the frame's former painting as a *Portrait of a Lady in a Broad-brimmed Hat* then clearly that is the end of your good provenance.

To be successful, all the above cookery or pickling, as an old teacher of mine used to call the patinating of pictures, requires judgement and skill, based on a long study of genuine old works. The first expert you will have to fool is yourself. When you have finished a work you must study it critically and ask yourself: 'If I were ignorant of this picture's origin, and it was brought to me for my appraisal, what date would I attach to it?' No matter how much it may go against the grain your answer must be an honest one. And only if you can tell yourself in all truthfulness that it would have fooled you into thinking it a genuine old painting is it likely to fool anybody else. For as the quotation of the head of this chapter tells us: 'It is in the ability to deceive oneself that the greatest talent is shown.'

PART THREE

Marketing

CHAPTER ELEVEN

The Expert

'What authority maintains today it generally contradicts tomorrow.'

HAROLD BAYLEY

Ever since St Jerome left the wilderness to set up home with his lion in a cosy Renaissance study there has been some confusion in the popular mind between saints and scholars. Like saints, scholars are expected to be guided in their actions by the highest moral principles, and when, on rare occasions, they let us down (as was the case when a highly respected medieval scholar stole three pages from a priceless manuscript in the Biblioteca Vaticana) our sense of disillusion is intense.

But, on the whole, scholars really do have saintly virtues, and of all the characters involved in the art world they are the most admirable. Seldom are they motivated by the vanity, avarice and pride that earmark so many collectors, dealers and artists for certain damnation. The average scholar quietly and disinterestedly pursues his studies to add patiently to our store of knowledge. Furthermore it is to him, more than anyone else, that we owe the organization of our great museums and the conservation of artistic treasures from the past.

Saintly as they are, experts do, however, sometimes make mistakes. Usually such errors are just that: mistakes not wrong-doings. Rarely do they deliberately make false attributions or knowingly 'authenticate' fakes. Nevertheless it is to the expert and his mistakes that we owe any authenticity that the works of art we have for sale may possess. For it is the expert, and only the expert, who is qualified to say whether or not our paintings and drawings are genuine. It is no use us telling them that we did or did not make the work that we are offering for their expertise. They are the experts, and they must and will decide. What we have to say does not count. Consequently, the first rule to be followed when offering works for a learned opinion is to keep quiet and leave the business of describing such works to the competence of the trained expert. Should they say your work is genuine then, at least for the time being, genuine it is. Equally if they say it is fake, fake it is.

Sometimes the verdict is made in the forger's favour and sometimes not. The same expert who has rejected one of our works may very well look kindly on another. Such was the experience of a talented artist and picture restorer, Theo van Wijngaarden. Sometime in the late twenties or early thirties Theo claimed to have discovered a painting in the style of Frans Hals. According to his story, when he came to clean the picture he used a far stronger solvent than he should have done, with the result that the paint softened. Knowing that one of the tests of an oil painting's age is the hardness of the paint, which can take over 50 years to dry out, Theo thought it the wisest course to admit his mistake to the authority on Frans Hals he had called in to examine his 'find'. The expert was impressed by the picture and having no reason to doubt Theo's word, authenticated the work. He even went so far as to introduce a buyer.

At this point, instead of leaving well alone, Theo sought a second opinion, this time from the renowned expert on Dutch pictures, Dr Abraham Bredius. The same scholar, incidentally, who in 1937 was to 'authenticate' van Meegeren's well-known *Disciples at Emmaus*, forged in the manner of Jan Vermeer (1632–75). To Theo's chagrin Dr Bredius took no notice of his explanation for the softened paint and rejected the work. Naturally the would-be buyer backed out, leaving the artist–restorer nursing a grudge. Theo was determined to get even with Bredius, and the following year saw him once again consulting the great man. This time he offered him a Rembrandt drawing for his inspection. Being totally convinced of its authenticity the scholar confirmed the attribution to Rembrandt. Whereupon Theo did something that must have made Bredius feel rather foolish: he tore the 'Rembrandt' to shreds before the expert's eyes.

To help the experts towards forming a favourable opinion of our efforts we have to know how their minds work. By definition a scholar is an intellectual. Intellectuals reason, and if we are to convince them that our work is genuine it must have its foundation in the same kind of reasoning as their own. We must learn to think like the expert and make an effort to present them works of art that correspond to their ideas rather than our own. That is to say we must satisfy their criteria as to what makes a genuine work of art whether or not we believe that criteria to be sound.

To begin to fathom the minds of our scholars, first let it be remembered that they are art historians. Their subject is a department of history and as such is governed by the same principles that govern the study of history in general. What, we may ask, are those principles? One might well imagine that the most important principle behind any good historical account must be veracity: surely the history must be a true one. In actual fact such a naive concept as telling the truth was dismissed by serious historians from the very start. The ancient historian, Herodotus (484 BC) makes the point very well when he writes: 'Very few things happen at the right time, and the rest do not happen at all! The conscientious historian will correct these things.' So conscientious were subsequent historians in making such corrections that, in our own era, Oscar Wilde was able to observe: 'To give an accurate description of what never happened is the proper occupation of the historian.'

What the art historian, along with all historians, attempts to do is give an appearance of order to what, in fact, never had any order. The way the art historian imposes order on to the lives and works of past artists is rather like the way the diligent gardener imposes order on his roses by tying them to a trellis: the trellis dictates the pattern of the plant's growth. The roses, left to themselves, ramble as they will; but on the grid of the trellis they reflect the ideas of tidy growth that the gardener thinks best for them. The basic laths of the trellis upon which artists and their work are forced by the historian are two. The first is composed of centuries: the fourteenth, fifteenth, sixteenth and so on; the second of schools: Italian, German, English, French or wherever the artist happened to have been born, lived or worked. According to this system artists and their works can be neatly labelled: seventeenth-century Dutch, eighteenth-century French or whatever seems appropriate. This is all very neat and tidy and makes the subject easy to teach, and it must be admitted that on the whole artists have been very obliging to the historian in this matter and have tried their very best to be born and to die within the same century without too much overlapping.

Should circumstances beyond their control have forced them out of line then at least they have normally been good enough to conform in their work to a particular school. Even so, there are always those exceptions who seem to be born and die whenever they think fit and to paint an draw in the manner of any school they please. If these rogues are minor artists then the art historian simply reaches for his pruning shears, but sometimes the artist is too important and likely to be missed. Take for instance van Dyck. Had he waited to be born for only one more year his dates (1599–1641) would have been exemplary; even so he fits neatly into the first half of the seventeenth century. But what about his style; what school does he belong to? Well, he was born in Flanders and studied under Rubens. He worked in Italy, where he painted in the manner of both the Genoese and the Neapolitan schools. He also worked in England, where he was court painter to Charles I and laid the foundation for the English school of portraiture that flowered in the eighteenth century (not a day earlier). These things considered, van Dyck has equal claim to belong to four different schools. This is awkward for the scholar, but the great artist can't be pruned away because of the importance of his influence on subsequent artists.

This brings me to another fallacy of art history, namely the notion of mainstream art. For art historians there are artists that count and artists that don't. Again the concept can be traced to the historian of our traditional history books. Writers who speak of kings, emperors, queens, statesmen and generals as though nobody else ever existed on this planet except as a background for these illustrious protagonists. Today the anthropologist has seriously called into question this myopic view of history, with the result that an entirely different picture is emerging of past ages, which, while not contradicting such facts as have been established by the old-fashioned historian, is beginning to round out our view of the past to include the greater part of mankind that was not composed of wealth and power. The art historian, however, has not kept up with the anthropologist and still clings to the notion of a few geniuses who somehow spring up from nowhere, unless it be from the influence of past superstars such as themselves.

This way of thinking is clearly illustrated by the art historian's account of modern art. For example any 'serious' history of contemporary British art will include certain names such as Henry Moore (1898–1986), Graham Sutherland (1903–80) and Francis Bacon (1909–92). One will also encounter the names of lesser lights who have worked along similar modernistic lines as these famous artists. One will, however, look in vain for the well-known names (in England) of such artists as Augustus John (1878–1961), Alfred Munnings (1878–1959) and Russell Flint (1880–1969), who were no less commercially successful than Moore, Sutherland and Bacon. The experts responsible for these histories would argue that the artists omitted from their account were not as good or as important to the mainstream of the Modern Movement as those mentioned. But surely it is not the historian's job to sit in judgement on the artists whose lives and work it is their business to chronicle. John, Munnings and Russell Flint existed. One may like their work or not, consider it anachronistic or not, but they are part of history. And surely it is bad history to be subjective about the matter. From an objective point of view bad guys are as much history as good guys. Imagine a historian of modern times cutting out of their account of the twentieth century Adolf Hitler, on the grounds of not happening to like him. The idea is ridiculous.

However that may be, we are getting a picture of the expert as a congenial manipulator both of history and taste, who must have everything just as he wants it. Our job is to satisfy his feelings in the matter. If he prefers some artists to other artists then those are the artists we will follow. If he wants pictures that fall neatly into schools and centuries then who are we to deny him the pleasure?

The criteria generally used by the expert to decide whether or not our work of art is really by a given master has been well stated by the Renaissance scholar Frederick Hartt, one of the most distinguished art historians of the twentieth century. A student of Bernard Berenson, Meyer Schapiro and Max Friedländer, he taught for more than 50 years, influencing generations of scholars. At the time of his death he was Paul Goodloe McIntire Professor Emeritus of the History of Art at the University of Virginia. Among many honours bestowed on him, he was a Knight of the Crown of Italy, a Knight Officer of the Order of Merit of the Italian Republic and an honorary citizen of Florence. I quote from the introduction of Dr Hartt's *The Drawings of Michelangelo* (London, 1971). Naturally he is speaking of drawings, but what he has to say is, with very little modification, the current criteria used for judging paintings as well.

By definition an imitation must lack the quality of the real thing...a copy, again by definition, is something made to resemble the original as closely as possible....All can easily be recognised as copies, due to their over careful halting line and soggy treatment of form.

Drawing is the most intimate of all modes of artistic expression, the immediate concretion of the artist's imagination and vision. The spontaneous movements of his hand cannot be accurately imitated in *shape* without destroying their *spontaneity*, nor can their *spontaneity* be emulated and the same shape retained. It can be stated with little fear of contradiction that no copyist can ever produce lines as crisp, free and sure, as those set down by the artist in the freshness of creation or observation. The artist works from imagination, memory, experience, emotion, impulse or any combination of these. The copyist can only try to set down exactly what he sees. In the copyist's version the artist's rapid line will inevitably slow down and wander a bit. The artist's shorthand, made only for himself, will be misunderstood by the copyist.

How about the *pentimenti*? The artist changes his mind half a dozen times before the pose is just right, or, even with the model sitting in front of him, before the contour of a limb flows the way he wants it to. Can the copyist make *pentimenti* too? Indeed he can, but his attempts to copy the artist's *pentimenti* will run the same risks as his efforts to reproduce any other line he did not invent. An artist's *pentimenti* are fresh, free and rapid, with clean, clear marks of the drawing tool held by a hand moving swiftly, without external controls. The copyist who has to look and draw, look and draw, cannot imitate this speed and freedom. His *pentimenti* will be about as convincing as a stage fall.'[52]

Fine words, and the majority of experts would agree with them, but are they true? Let us make a list of Dr Hartt's four major assumptions or premises and see if they can be shown to be undeniably sound and invariably applicable.

1. An imitation must lack the quality of the real thing.
2. A copy is something made to resemble the original as closely as possible.
3. All copies can easily be recognized for what they are, due to their over-careful halting line and soggy treatment of form.
4. No copyist can ever produce lines as crisp, free, and as sure, as those set down by the artist in the freshness of creation or observation.

The four assumptions all stem from one apparent, if unstated, premise, namely that copyists are not artists. If this premise is unsound then all four assumptions upon which the scholars' criteria for judging the authenticity of drawings collapse.

The simplest way of testing the truth or otherwise of the statement 'copyists are not artists' is to reverse it. This is because logic tells us that if X is not Y, Y cannot be X, from which it follows that if copyists are not artists, then artists cannot be copyists. That this last statement is false is at once made plain by listing the names of a few copyists whose claim to being artists is indisputable. In this book alone we mention Michelangelo, Andrea del Sarto (1486–1530), Rembrandt, Rubens, Goya, Turner, Delacroix, Degas and other distinguished copyists. True, these artists would not be as famous as they are if they had only been copyists, but this is beside the point. All we want to know is whether copyists can be artists, and the answer is a resounding yes!

This established, we may point to thousands of examples that show Dr Hartt's own thesis to be about as 'convincing as a stage fall'. Let one example to undermine each of his four assumptions suffice:

1. Andrea del Sarto's copy of Raphael's portrait of *Pope Julius II* does not lack the quality of the original.
2. Rembrandt's copy of Holbein's drawing of an English lady (*see* plate 19) has not been made to resemble the original as closely as possible.
3. Rubens' copy of Leonardo's *Battle of Anghiari* does not show an overcareful halting line and soggy treatment of form.
4. Goya's copy, or adaptation, of Flaxman's outline (*see* plates 35 and 36) does not show lines any less free and sure than the work from which he is stealing. Indeed it is the original that is lacking these qualities.

At this point it is clear that there are both good copies, versions and adaptations worthy of being called art, and bad ones that can make no such claim. The scholar's criteria, as set down by Hartt, will sort out only the bad ones. This being so we must attempt to make our drawings:

1. of the same quality as our model;
2. not necessarily to resemble the original as closely as possible;
3. free of halting lines and soggy forms;
4. contain lines as free and sure as those set down by an artist in the freshness of creation or observation.

Our success or otherwise depends on the extent to which we achieve these aims, which is, of course, also the extent to which we ourselves may claim to be artists.

No portrait of the expert, however sketchy it may be, should lack mention of his extraordinary capacity – once the prerogative of ladies – to change his mind. This intellectual flexibility is undoubtedly a virtue. What is disturbing, however, is that once certain ideas are discarded they are rarely revisited, and it is always the latest idea that is considered the right one. This is largely due to the fact that the champions of old ideas are usually dead, and the new ideas do not find the opposition they should have to test their validity. A good instance of this is afforded by the recent reattributions surrounding Rembrandt's work. At the beginning of the century the number of paintings in public and private collections attributed to Rembrandt was in the region of 1000. Today the number has dwindled to less than 300. This is largely the result of the labours of an all-Dutch committee of experts set up and financed by their government to reassess Rembrandt's work and, where they think necessary, to reattribute pictures to such painters working in the master's circle, such as: Dou, Bol, Drost, Flinck, van Hoogstraten and van den Eeckhout.

Nowadays, according to the committee, the Wallace Collection in London, which once owned twelve Rembrandts, has only one. The National Gallery of London has lost one in three of its former fifteen Rembrandts and Her Majesty Queen Elizabeth has lost three out of seven. The Metropolitan Museum of New York has four Rembrandt casualties, as does the Duke of Westminster.

Naturally the reattributed pictures have lost much of their former monetary value. The portrait of a *Bearded Man*, formerly in the Thyssen-Bornemisza Collection and once valued at £4.5 million, recently changed hands at a tenth of that price. Perhaps the most staggering drop in value is that suffered by Rembrandt's famous masterpiece, *The Polish Rider*. This picture was acquired by the Pittsburgh industrialist Henry Clay Frick and left to the American nation, together with other treasures, housed in the Frick mansion-museum in New York City. Although not for sale, the estimated value of *The Polish Rider* when a Rembrandt was £35 million. Now, as a Drost, dealers are speaking of £1 million.

If these pictures have lessened in monetary value, they have lost nothing in artistic value. Furthermore, given the fact that new experts are always happy to disagree with former ones, the downgraded works may yet be reinstated as works from Rembrandt's own hand.

One demoted work, which, in my opinion (and in the opinion of many other art lovers), deserves to be reattributed to Rembrandt himself is a very beautiful little panel picture in the National Gallery, London. This painting, formerly known as *The Philosopher* is now boringly described as a *Man in a*

Room, painted by 'an imitator of Rembrandt' (*see* plate 51). I could speak at length of the artistic virtues of this picture, of its splendid composition, of its amazing quality of light, of its brilliant handling and much else. All that, however, would be put down by the picture's detractors to my lack of judgement, a lack of judgement I share with the generations of art lovers who have viewed *The Philosopher* as one of the joys of the National Gallery's Rembrandt Room. So I shall leave aside any further mention of the picture's great merits and speak of how the former attribution to Rembrandt is strongly supported by scientific evidence. Proof that the Rembrandt revisionists have chosen to ignore.

In the thirties *The Philosopher* was examined by Dr A. P. Laurie as Professor of Chemistry at the Royal Academy of Arts, London. Professor Laurie had introduced a very convincing method for separating Rembrandt's work from that of his followers, which he published under the title of *The Brushwork of Rembrandt and his School*. Essentially his thesis is this:

> The drawing with the brush of each painter differs more markedly than men's signatures differ from one another. The brushwork of any given artist is more clearly seen in full impasto, and full impasto is a marked feature of such great seventeenth-century painters as Velasquez, Frans Hals and Rembrandt.

If we compare one with another, Velasquez with Hals, for instance, and Hals with Rembrandt, we find that each has his own individual brushwork, which is common to his pictures, but quite alien to those of his two great colleagues (*see* plates 50, 52 and 53). Professor Laurie writes:

> As in writing, once a painter has formed his style of brushwork, it is curiously persistent. His pictures may alter with the years; they may develop a greater depth of meaning and richer quality, as we find with Rembrandt, but the brushwork remains the same.

Starting from the premise that painters who do not smooth out their brushwork are signing their work with every stroke, Professor Laurie set about photographing the paintings of Rembrandt and his school with 'a camera capable of considerable extension and with the movements of a microscope'. By these means he obtained microphotographs of various details of the pictures under examination. These enlarged the details from one and a half to two diameters, sometimes as much as five, revealing every stroke of the brush with the utmost definition.

Professor Laurie then proceeded to use the microphotographs in the following way (I quote from his book *New Light on Old Masters* (1935):

> If we now proceed to take silver prints of the magnified photographs of two pictures, one, (whose authorship is known and the other unknown, and cutting up the one, put a portion on the other print so adjusted that the strokes of the brush follow on, we have an infallible method of identification. As examples of this method, I can mention the horse's mane in [Rembrandt's] the *Good Samaritan* of 1633, and the nose of *Titus* of about 1657, matched with the bodice of the *Woman Taken in Adultery* of 1644. It is inconceivable that any other hand could have reproduced so exactly the reticulated paint surface revealed in these three pictures.[53]

Professor Laurie goes on to explain that the above-mentioned photographs were taken to prove conclusively that a Dr Martin was mistaken in thinking that the *Good Samaritan* was not by Rembrandt.

Were Professor Laurie with us today he would certainly uphold the attribution to Rembrandt of the National Gallery's former *Philosopher*. This is because when he took microphotographs of details from the painting he was impressed by 'how the effect of the structure of the wooden frame of the window and the light on the broken plaster is obtained by a dragged impasto of white lead over dark underlying paint, exactly repeated in the *Good Samaritan*',[54] thus proving that the two paintings are by the same artist.

If the artist who painted *The Philosopher* was not Rembrandt, then nor is the *Good Samaritan*, the *Titus* or the *Woman Taken in Adultery* by Rembrandt. And we can by the same token continue to dismiss all pictures with this kind of brushwork from Rembrandt's oeuvre until we finally throw out the celebrated *Night Watch* itself. Then we find ourselves in the absurd position of having to postulate a genius other than Rembrandt who has painted this body of masterworks and join those crackpots of the kind who attribute Shakespeare's works to Marlowe, Bacon and others.

Surely it would be more sensible to reinstate *The Philosopher*, which would bring back in its trail so many of those masterpieces that for so long added lustre to the name of Rembrandt. It is time for the *Polish Rider* to ride right back into the forefront of the master's work – although it must be admitted that for many of us it never rode out.

Like Rembrandt, Michelangelo also suffered from over-zealous revision-ists. These clever people removed all the master's highly finished 'presenta-tion' drawings from his oeuvre, together with many of the most magnificent studies from the Sistine Chapel. Luckily a new generation of scholars reinstated the works, and for the time being we are allowed to enjoy them as works by Michelangelo himself. But, beware of the next bunch of experts.

Let us, however, be thankful for the expert, for without his blessing there would be no authentic work at all. Sometimes he may irritate us, as Bernard Berenson once irritated Ioni. The faker had taken, for Berenson's opinion, a genuine panel picture from the fourteenth century. The great scholar would not see Ioni face to face, and the painter was obliged to stand outside his study while the picture was taken in by a secretary. On seeing the painting Berenson said in a loud voice, 'Tell Signor Ioni he is getting better as a faker.' At which Ioni replied in an even louder voice, 'Ah, it's always the same, when I bring him a fake it becomes genuine, and when I bring him a genuine work it becomes fake!' Nevertheless, on the whole, the expert is our greatest ally in making our work saleable. That he occasionally makes mis-takes is all to our advantage, and the best experts would say with journalist James Gordon Bennett: 'I have made mistakes, but I have never made the mistake of claiming I have never made one.'

Following this chapter on the expert we are to speak of the dealer and it might be an appropriate link between the two chapters to mention the experts who work for the dealers. In this particular case, Phillips the fine-art auctioneers. The following extract is from the diaries of Alan Clark,[55] the son and heir of the renowned connoisseur Lord Clark of Saltwood:

Saltwood   *Sunday, 2 October*

The place is full of Phillips' employees, doing an inventory. They shuffle about amiably, opening cupboards and chests, peeping and poking. I'm amazed at how ignorant they are. I mean some of them have specialised knowledge, of course, which I can't match on porcelain or silver or 'gems'. But most of them give the impression of learning as they go along. There's that mysterious greenish picture that hangs over the fireplace in the red study; the man from the Getty (I can't remember his name and he's been sacked since coming here) said it was a Bellini; v. unlikely, I feel, but it is important. The 'paintings expert' looked at it for a bit, literally scratching his head, finally said to Jane, 'Did Lord Clark ever meet Bernard Berenson?'

[Lord Clark worked under Berenson in Florence for three years after leaving Oxford. They remained close friends and colleagues for the next fifty years.]

So different from real enthusiasts like Peter Wilson, or Byam Shaw. Something would catch their eye and they would look at it for ages, and really love it. What was it worth? Oh nothing really, two or three hundred pounds, but that didn't matter, the point is they *loved* it. Christie's are the worst. What I really object to is the way that they *sneer* at the stuff as they go round: we don't mind slumming occasionally, but tee-hee, look at this, how quaint, nothing like the one in the Frick, etc, etc. Sotheby's are jollier but they charge. And anyway, I don't want them to know what I've got here. No one's got into the keep before, and I'm only doing this at the behest of the Revenue. With a bit of luck some of Phillips's definitions will be sufficiently imprecise as to be untraceable.

CHAPTER TWELVE

The Dealer

'He who reaps the profits has committed the crime.'

SENECA

Although art dealers existed in ancient times, and some firms claim to have been in business for centuries, the dealer as we know him today is really the product of art collecting on both sides of the Atlantic in the nineteenth and twentieth centuries.

After the end of the American Civil War in 1865 the art market there boomed, much as it was to do again after the Second World War. The quality of the pictures changing hands scarcely seemed to matter, and providing they were not 'primitives', they could be new or old, good or bad, American or European. If quality were of no importance, subject-matter was, and this aspect of the trade was amusingly discussed by a contemporary auctioneer writing in *Harper's* in 1860. Calling himself 'Smith'[56] and his partner 'Stipples', he tells us that they possessed the five essential virtues for selling pictures: they were to be 'good looking, of good address and gentle manners, with great flow of language and impudence unbounded'. Having collected 'a lot of very poor paintings', 'Smith & Stipples' opened a third-floor gallery backing on to Broadway. Prospective customers willing to climb the stairs were found to be so many that the partners decided to charge an entrance fee, but finding that the 25-cent charge 'extinguished the crowd' they soon dropped it. A guided tour of the gallery was conducted by Stipples, who 'having crammed for art talk from a manual on the subject' was able to come up with some suitably impressive phrases.

After two years of selling old portraits to 'Western gentlemen' in need of ancestors together with other 'cast-iron paintings', Smith & Stipples decided to turn their premises into an auction house. Business was brisk, and the partners began to learn much about what would and what would not sell. Smith tells us:

> It is the picture that tells a story that I like most and sells best. Cattle and sheep have often given me a great deal of trouble. Pigs are generally more in demand. One cow looking over another cow's back is very well liked, and a terrier looking out of a hole is good for a certain sum.

Stipples was in charge of the 'Old Masters', and it was in this department that his eloquence blossomed. On one occasion, when trying to sell a picture that Smith describes as 'the worst picture I ever saw in our auction rooms and utterly worthless', his partner gave it the following build-up:

> Ladies and gentlemen, it is not more than once in a century that such a painting as this is exhibited. The owner, a gentleman of enormous wealth (sensation and awe in the audience), would have taken it with him to Europe, where he resides ten months of the year, had he not hesitated to deprive the country of so valuable a work of art. I hope that his patriotic motives will be appreciated by you (applause). The subject, the *Landing of the Pilgrims*, is one of the noblest in the world, and the treatment is – but it would be presumptuous of me to praise the work of the man who painted it. When I mention the name of Squilgee you will understand my diffidence. I may point out to you, however, one or two points in the picture in which the artist has excelled himself. That blasted tree in the foreground is an exquisite bit of painting. The short herbage beneath it is crisp and juicy. ... You will also observe the prismatic effect of the light on the background ... but I need not direct your attention to what must be so obvious to the crowd of art judges before me.

Stipples concluded his sales talk by saying: 'An opportunity is now offered for someone here to become the owner of one of the greatest paintings of modern times.' But even such gifts of oratory could not sell the unsaleable, and the painting was knocked down to a bogus buyer for $400.

At the beginning of this century wealthy American collectors discovered the allure of old Europe and, with it, Europe's Old Masters. This was the time when J. P. Morgan was bent on making his collection of Old Master pictures the greatest personal collection in the world. Joseph Duveen bought Gainsborough's *Blue Boy* from the Duke of Westminster and sold it to Henry

E. Huntingdon of San Marino, California, for $620,000. Dealers in Old Master paintings and drawings were enjoying a prosperity they had never seen before.

Then came the depression of the thirties, and with it the passing of the old-style tycoon and the approach of depersonalized business in the form of the corporation. To a large extent the corporation took over from the tycoon the collecting and patronizing of art, but obviously an impersonal body cannot have the personal passion for collecting that drove individuals such as Morgan, William Randolph Hearst, P. A. B. Widener and Paul Mellon to form their great collections. The purpose of a corporation is to make money, not to cultivate taste in art. Taste is desirable only in so far as it is tax deductible. The most beautiful picture in the world, as one sales executive put it, is a sales curve bending upwards. And it is this picture that the dealer must supply if he wishes to enjoy a similarly attractive work of art on his own walls.

So it has come about that we now see the more important dealers in the guise of corporate businessmen able to justify all the tricks of their trade, provided they are performed in the hallowed name of business. But no matter how they present themselves, one has only to catch them off guard, and there they stand, those charming rogues of yore: Messrs Smith & Stipple. It was this kind of dealer that Augusto Jandolo, himself one of the tribe, had in mind when he wrote:

A dealer's life would provide the writer with an endless supply of hilarious material. Shrewd plans matured over long periods in utter seclusion and secrecy, craftily concocted frauds of the most subtle or impudent character end in situations that Boccaccio might have contrived. When such deceptions are sooner or later brought to light, they send half the world into paroxysms of rage or laughter.

What has been said above gives a kind of basic anatomy of the dealer, where variations have been disregarded in the interest of a basic understanding of the type. The faker attempting to dispose of his wares will not, however, be confronted with a type but with an individual. At one end of the scale will stand an amusing, charming, educated individual, as honest as can be. At the other, a sullen, scheming ignorant rogue, Here, I hasten to add, what I intend by scale has nothing whatsoever to do with social or business standing. The charming reputable dealer may be running a junk shop, the sullen rogue may be the chairman of an auction house.

There are four classes of dealer with whom we may from time to time do business: the junk dealer, the antique dealer, the picture dealer and the auctioneer.

The Junk Dealer

The junk dealer is a very useful outlet for disposing of our failures. Quality doesn't matter here, so obviously one does not offer anything that might conceivably interest a better market. As a rule, the junk dealer knows very little about art and is more likely to be able to appraise a rusty spoon or some other object of scrap metal than an 'Old Master'.

Nevertheless he has heard that pictures can fetch high prices, and being eager for a profit he will normally be prepared to risk a few pounds. This is always providing you can convince him that:

1. the picture is a hand-painted original;
2. it was left to you by a wealthy aunt who always said it was worth a fortune;
3. you don't have the bus fare to take it to Sotheby's.

Once convinced that he might be getting a bargain the dealer may ask you how much you want for the work. Knowing that whatever you ask he is going to say is too much, you calculate the lowest figure you would accept and double it. If, on the other hand, the dealer should make an offer, you again multiply by two to get a rough idea of the highest sum he is prepared to pay. If your haggling is successful you should end up with enough money to cover the cost of your materials and buy a few drinks at the pub to get you into a positive mood, determined to do better next time.

A word of warning: before attempting to cut your losses by selling your failures to the rag-and-bone merchant, you must remember that in all probability he will later have it vetted by somebody higher up in the hierarchy of dealers. This is dangerous, because when it is discovered to be 'not right' (as failures must) it may give some expert somewhere an example of your handiwork to use for comparison with your better efforts, following in the same style, therefore jeopardizing the success of your future productions. A safe alternative to the junk dealer for the disposal of your failures is the rubbish bin.

The Antique Dealer

The dealer in general antiques offers an excellent market for our decorative fakes, that is to say those pictures we have made in the style of past masters to please and yet with no intention of passing expert scrutiny. You will have chosen an attractive subject, executed it in an agreeable manner and given it such signs of age that are necessary to make it fit seamlessly into a period setting.

Care should be taken when offering your work to an antique dealer that the picture is in keeping with their other stock. You will normally be well on the way to achieving this aim because according to an antique dealer of my acquaintance, 80 per cent of all antiques on the market today are just like your decorative picture, that is decorative fakes. They, too, have been made to satisfy a taste for objects of the past at a reasonable price. But, even so, it is a waste of time to offer delicate miniatures to a dealer in large, imposing objects intended for the decoration of hotel foyers, or acres of forceful canvas to a dealer in charming bric-à-brac for the small home. So before offering your wares to an antique dealer it is wise to examine their stock carefully before ringing their bell.

Some dealers in decorative 'antiques' describe their goods honestly, calling them reproductions, replicas or whatever, others are less candid. But honest or otherwise, being merchants, they are less concerned with the age, authorship or quality of your picture than its saleability. If unsaleable to their particular clientele they will turn it down. If they can see money in it for themselves you have made a sale. Incidentally, a number of dealers in reproduction furniture and *objets d'art* employ artists of our kind on a regular basis. On the whole they pay fair prices and must be regarded as among the faker's best customers.

The Picture Dealer

When we offer our wares to a dealer who specializes in drawings and paintings we are often challenging a very knowledgeable person who may be considered as an expert as well as a merchant, especially by themselves. This being the case it is well to treat the art dealer as one would the scholar. This advice – so easy to give – reminds me of a skit on a manual dealing with taxidermy, which, under the heading of 'Elephant', had: 'Treat as for mole purse.'

Certainly, trying to do business with a rapacious dealer is a much more harrowing affair than speaking with the gentle, disinterested scholar! Nevertheless, basically, it's the same technique. That is, keep quiet and let them decide what it is you have for sale.

The best possible way of introducing yourself to a dealer is as a customer. Dealers adore customers, and once you have achieved this status you will always be given a warm welcome. Buying from them also ensures that you will get to know their stock, what kind of pictures they like and what prices they ask for them. This last point is very important because it will help you to establish their mark-up. Dealers generally get a good proportion of their stock from the auction rooms, and if you have been following the salerooms' activities you are quite likely to see something on their walls sold recently at auction. Consequently you know that they paid for it.

Another way of getting to know a dealer (and in any case better than just walking in off the street) is to pretend they have been recommended to you by some important person in the trade or in the museum world as being the most likely person to advise you about your picture and how to sell it. A little flattery goes a long way with dealers. By the same token they are very touchy about criticism. Twice in my misspent youth I was foolish enough to imply a criticism of a dealer's knowledge; in both cases I was trying to prevent them from making a mistake.

The first time was at an exhibition of important Old Master drawings held in London's West End. One of the drawings on show was attributed to G.B. Tiepolo. It was a very good drawing, but there was something about it that seemed alien to Tiepolo's drawing style, as far as I knew it from my limited experience. As I was examining the work, trying to discover what it was that was worrying me, I was rewarded with proof positive that the drawing was not Tiepolo's. The composition, which represented the Holy Family, contained a column on which were discreetly inscribed the initials of the true author of the work, S.R. – Sebastiano Ricci (1659–1734). It was one of Ricci's very close approaches to Tiepolo. By the way, Ricci was famous for his brilliant fakes of Veronese (1528–88). When I pointed out his error to the dealer he went blind with rage. So blind he couldn't see the initials and showed me at once to the door. Ricci is, of course, worth less than Tiepolo. The next time I saw the drawing I couldn't myself see Ricci's initials. In their place was a slightly roughened area of paper where they had been scraped away.

The second time I made the mistake of being a do-gooder was many years

ago at a sale of Old Masters at Christie's in Rome. The picture was described
in a catalogue as a gouache by Gianpaolo Panini (c.1692–1765): it was a
splendid architectural view of excellent quality. What was wrong with the
painting was the fact that one of our colleagues had painted it on top of an
old engraving and had inadvertently left one or two slight traces of the
engraving showing through. These traces could scarcely be seen by the
naked eye unless one knew for what one was looking. As I was examining
the picture two young dealers of my acquaintance (let us call them Smith &
Stipple Jr) asked me what I thought of it; telling me in the same breath that
they thought it was wonderful and were intent on buying it. This should
have warned me not to contradict their opinion. Instead, thinking that I
would do them a good turn and save them from losing their money, I told
them what I had discovered. At this they got very cross and told me that I
didn't know what I was talking about. When the 'Panini' lot came under the
hammer the bidding was brisk, and the two dealers had to pay a stiff price
for it. After the sale I spoke to one of Christies' staff and, congratulating the
firm on the good prices realized, mentioned that of the 'Panini'. 'I'm afraid
that lot was not a real sale – it was bought in,' said the Christie's man. 'But,'
said I, 'I saw 'Smith & Stipples' run the price up to 7 million lire.' 'Yes, that's
exactly what they did; they were running up the price on their own property
and got landed with it!' was the answer.

What happened, of course, was this. Young 'Smith & Stipples' knew perfectly well that the Panini was a fake (they had probably commissioned it
themselves with a particular customer in mind) and had put it into the sale
for two reasons, neither of which was to sell it. One was to establish a
good provenance and the other to establish a high value. After paying the
auctioneers their commission, all they had to do was to show the prospective
customer the Christie's catalogue and the 'Panini' could confidently be offered
on the strength of the auctioneer's expertise and their own apparent will-
ingness to pay a good price for it. Naturally the person they had been bidding
against was a stooge hired for the purpose. It is difficult to imagine how an
obvious fake of this kind, one painted over an old print, could have deceived
Christie's. The only explanation I can think of is that the Panini expert
consulted had only a photograph from which to judge. Whatever the truth
of the matter, my fear of the two young dealers losing their money was
unfounded. Clearly they are worthy chips off the old Smith & Stipples block
and are still flourishing a quarter of a century later.

In 1949 Russell Lynes wrote of American art dealers in these terms:

Art dealing is free enterprise in its most lively dog-eat-dog manifestations. The only noticeable solidarity among dealers in America is geographical; more than 90 per cent of our important art merchants cluster on or near Fifty Seventh street in New York. Fifty Seventh street is not known for its *bonhomie*. Unlike other kinds of merchants, art dealers have no general association to look out for their interests, to adjudicate their differences and to keep a protecting eye on their practices. They are more like the members of an Oriental bazaar than like American merchants. The delicacy of their relationships, the suspicion, rivalry and secrecy among them is such that any sort of cooperative organization is unthinkable.[57]

Such was the situation immediately after the Second World War in the United States. In England, however, in addition to the geographical solidarity afforded by the West End of London in general, and Old and New Bond Street in particular, there has for long been an association of the 'better' type of dealers. The association of which I speak is not BADA, the British Antique Dealers' Association, but the OBC, the Old Boys' Club. This is a kind of Mafia, organized by ex-'public' schoolboys who manipulate London's art market from the top. Their method is as simple as it is effective. They simply squeeze out competition by snobbery. They and they alone are gentlemen and scholars. They alone are totally reputable. Their holier-than-thou attitude allows them to make and break the rules of the game just as they think fit. When some outsider falls into disgrace over some shady deal the humbugs are the first to moralize and publicly condemn, but when one of themselves is discovered to have departed from the path of honesty they swiftly close ranks to defend the culprit. Italians, dealers and public, seem to have a more realistic attitude to the whole business of dishonesty and morality. When the English papers are, let us say, having a field day because some well-known politician has been discovered sleeping with his secretary, the average Italian says: 'So what! Politicians do on occasion sleep with their secretaries – this is a fact of life.' Similarly it is understood that art dealers are on occasion dishonest. An Italian would probably term it shrewd. The law protects the collector up to a point, but, in general, the Italian's sympathy is for the miscreant rather than the victim. The former is considered *furbo* (smart) and the second *fesso* (stupid). Buyer beware is the motto. Nevertheless the dealer must not be found out, because that would be *poco furbo* (not very smart). In short, the Italian idea of an honest dealer is one who has never been caught. And this is certainly a fair definition of the many dealers who are only honest when honesty happens to be the best policy.

The Auctioneer

Of the various channels open to us for the selling of our 'Old Masters', the saleroom is possibly the best. This is largely due to the fact that auctioneers are absolute specialists in selling fakes. Naturally they have an enormous turnover of genuine items, but experience has shown them that however careful they may be in describing the goods that pass through their rooms there is, and always will be, a number of drawings and paintings that do not exactly fit the expert's description of them in the relevant sale catalogue.

This being the case every saleroom protects its interest by making conditions of sale to shield them from the ire of customers who may later discover that their pictures are not what they hoped. After telling the would-be buyer that every care has been taken to ensure that any statement as to authorship, attribution, origin, date, age, provenance and condition is reliable and accurate, the notice in their sales catalogues normally hasten to add that 'all such statements are merely statements of opinion and are not to be taken as representations of fact.' Then follows some such standard conditions of sale as:

> All lots are sold as shown, with all faults, imperfections and errors of description. Neither the auctioneers, nor the vendor [us] are responsible for such errors of description or of the genuineness or authenticity of any lot, or for any fault or defect in it. No warranty whatsoever is given by the auctioneers, or any vendor to any buyer in respect of any lot.

Excellent! This covers the interests of both the auctioneers and ourselves, and we can sell our fakes with impunity. Nevertheless, any disappointed buyer can, if they act quickly enough, get their money back, because notwithstanding the conditions set out above, another condition in the sale catalogue will normally say something to this effect:

> If within a certain period of time [normally 21 days] of the sale of any lot the buyer gives notice in writing to the auctioneer that the lot sold is a forgery and if within 14 days of giving such notice the buyer returns the lot in the same condition as it was at the time of the sale, and shows that,

considered in the light of the terms of the catalogue, the lot sold is a forgery, the auctioneers will rescind the sale and refund the purchase price received by them.

The important salerooms are not easily taken in by fakes and normally indicate their doubts about any given lot by the use of a code in the catalogue entry. If, for instance, they give the artist's name in full, it indicates that they feel that the work is by that master. If, however, they give only the initials of his first names then there is some doubt in their minds as to the artist. But if they print only the surname then it indicates that the work is almost certainly not by that artist and of 'uncertain' date, and the prospective buyer must understand that they are probably being offered a Vincent van Blank.

All this is marvellous for us. Here we have a more or less invulnerable front, where even our worst productions can be sold with the surname of some master attached to it. Our rewards may be great or small, but the solicitors who framed the salerooms' conditions of sale have protected our interests, and we have not transgressed the law.

You will already have had some experience of the saleroom as a buyer of unimportant lots for use as material for producing better things. So the general procedure is known to you, and I need say little of it here. In the more important salerooms in London there are usually numbers of attractive young people milling around who have just graduated in art history from some university or other. Pretty as they mostly are, they are visually speaking as ignorant as swans, and this is very irritating indeed. In fact nothing could be more annoying to us forgers than being faced with the so-called expert who can't even recognize what it is we have tried to fake.

My first experience of this was with Christie's, back in the sixties. I had made for the saleroom's perusal a set of six drawings in the manner of Goya. They were in red chalk and on eighteenth-century paper. The darling curly-headed young man responsible for cataloguing them hadn't got the foggiest idea of what he was looking at; after minutes of indecision he nodded his locks and told me he would have to consult the expert on nineteenth-century French drawings. Eventually the catalogue entry read: 'French school, nine-teenth century, close to Forain.' The reserve suggested by the auctioneers was only £10. To put matters right I hit on the plan of telling a bargain hunter who I knew to be attending the sale that what looked like six Goyas had been incorrectly catalogued as being French. He checked the works against Goya's published drawings and finding them closer to Goya than to Forain ran the bidding up to the then sizable sum of £200.

On another occasion I offered to Sotheby's a perfectly genuine drawing connected with a well-known picture in the Gallerie dell'Accademia in Venice from the workshop of Gentile Bellini. The drawing had formerly been attributed by two distinguished scholars to Antonio Pisanello (c.1395–c.1455), and there was no doubt that it was from the fifteenth century. Notwithstanding this, the charming young lady fresh from the Courtauld insisted that my drawing was sixteenth century. I could have throttled her. Disposing of dealers and experts in this way is, however, not done, and here follows a list of other dos and don'ts that may help you to deal with dealers.

Do

1. Dress appropriately. What is appropriate for a visit to a junk shop may be frowned upon elsewhere.
2. Be on time. If you have made an appointment keep it punctually, or the dealer will be ill disposed towards you or anything you might show him.
3. Accept his opinion. If he doesn't like your work try to learn from his criticism.

Don't

1. Tell the dealer his business. Gentle persuasion may sometimes be used, but remember he knows far better than you what he can or cannot sell.
2. Criticize his premises or his stock. If you can't find anything pleasant to say about them, say nothing.
3. Talk art. Talk money instead. You may feel out of your depth, but money (however modest the sum) is why you are visiting the dealer in the first place.
4. Describe your picture. Unless you happen to have a degree in art history you are not qualified to give an opinion as to its age, quality or authorship.

Postscript

In case art dealers should feel I have been unfair in what I have said of their trade in this chapter, I shall let them have the last word. Here is a self-appraisal, taken from the foreword by Giancarlo Gallino, Chairman of the

Piemonte Antique Dealer's Association, to 1995's gold-covered catalogue of the biannual antiques fair in Turin:

I have already had occasion to repeat how the noble profession of the antique dealer, when practised in a competent and correct manner, raises our consciousness of culture, encourages the habit of collecting, and teaches respect and sensitivity for our cultural heritage.

CHAPTER THIRTEEN

The Collector

'Art hath an enemy called ignorance.'

BEN JONSON

O n the whole the collector is a maligned creature. Some would blame him for the very existence of fakes: 'It is the demand that creates the supply' is the shallow argument. In addition for being blamed for our sins, the collector is lumbered with a number of unpleasant epithets: gullible, greedy and vain being three of the most common, it being quite forgotten that gullibility, greed and vanity are tribal traits, which, in differing degrees, we all possess. And what of those great collectors whose connoisseurship and love of art have saved so many beautiful things from neglect or destruction? Those men of consummate taste who devoted their lives to the gathering of artistic treasures for no more selfish a purpose than to leave them to our public galleries and museums, where they may now be enjoyed by everyone?

No, collecting in itself can be a highly commendable activity. Unfortunately, however, it all too often attracts the wrong kind of people: those who see it as a means of showing off, investing their money, buying prestige, or obtaining other ends far removed from the simple enjoyment of art. These collectors are the ones who deserve to be criticized or even ridiculed. Indeed, ever since the time of ancient Rome they have been a target for satire, and a glance at some past collectors, historical and fictional, reveals the following menagerie.

The Peacock
We all know this vain, strutting type. He is the Pauleus of whom the poet

Martial remarks: 'His friends, like his paintings and his antiques, all for show'. As his brain is very much smaller than his tail, the peacock is very likely to make a Trimalchio of himself. This well-known, parvenu millionaire character from Petronius's *Satyricon* is in the habit of forcing his dinner guests to admire his priceless possessions, telling them that his Corinthian vases (naturally the finest in the world) were commissioned directly from the great artist Corinth. He also possessed a cup decorated with a bas-relief representing Cassandra murdering her children.

A peacock of my acquaintance is the proud owner of a portrait of one of her 'eighteenth-century' ancestors wearing a bowler-hat and a collar and tie.

The Vulture

René Gimpel, in his *Diary of an Art Dealer* (1963; Eng. trans. London, 1966), recalls how the famous bibliophile Gallimard told him of how he had assembled his splendid collection of nineteenth-century wood-engravings. The moment Gallimard learnt of the death of any engraver of note he would be on the deceased's doorstep to haggle over buying whatever prints the dead man had left. 'I'd rush round to his widow or see his family and buy the complete works,' he said. And then he added with a note of pride, his eye sparkling with satisfaction: 'I've made good use of my opportunities.' Gimpel, commenting on this vulture's revelations, concluded: 'What a book could be written on the cruelty of the collector.'

The Wolf

The cruelty of collectors to collectors gave rise to this version of an old Latin phrase by Edmond Bonaffé: *Homo homini lupus, femina feminae lupior, curiosus curio lupissimus,* which may be freely rendered in English as: Man against man is like a wolf, woman against woman even more so, but the most wolflike of all is collector against collector.

Among the most wolflike of collectors, ancient or modern, the rapacious Roman senator Verres surely heads the pack. Voracious as he was he seems to have been a connoisseur, looting only what met his standards. Cicero, to whose *In Verrem* we owe the merciless indictment of Verres, tells us that, when proconsul in Sicily, Verres looted every temple on the island:

I defy you to find now in Sicily, this rich province, so old, with opulent families and cities, a single vase, a bronze of Corinth or Delos, one single precious stone or pearl, a single work in gold or ivory, a single bronze, marble or ivory statue; I defy you to find a single painting, a tapestry, that Verres has not been after, examined, and if pleasing to him, pillaged. His rapacity does not stop there. Should he learn of some fine work of art in private hands he was totally unscrupulous and would not hesitate to employ torture to extort the desired object. Even when invited to supper by friends he was known to have scraped some particularly fine bas-reliefs off the silver plates and hidden them in the folds of his toga.

Another wolf of ancient Rome, and one wielding greater power than Verres, was Mark Anthony, who demanded from Verres, as a forced gift, certain vases of Corinthian bronze. But Verres was so attached to his plunder that he preferred to face death rather than hand them over.

The Squirrel

This creature is a compulsive hoarder. He may hoard valuable works of art or he may hoard rubbish, but hoard he must. To this type of collector the individual item scarcely counts at all. He seldom really appreciates a work of art for its intrinsic value, it is just one more nut on the pile. A classic example of this animal is Sir Thomas Phillips (1792–1872). His vast hoard was perhaps the largest collection of books and manuscripts ever brought together by one person. It was his express aim to have 'one copy of every book in the world'. At his death Phillips left behind well over 120,000 items, including not only books and manuscripts but also charts, maps, seals, letters and Old Master drawings. During the more than 120 years since his death, Sotheby's have held 60 sales of 'The Celebrated Collection of Sir Thomas Phillips'. How this squirrel lived to satisfy his passion has been vividly recorded by Sir Frederick Madden, then keeper of manuscripts at London's British Museum, who writes in his diary of a visit to Sir Thomas's home, Middle Hill, in the summer of 1854.

The house looks more miserable and dilapidated every time I visit it, and there is not a room now that is not crowded with large boxes full of MSS. The state of things is really inconceivable. Lady P. is absent, and, were I in her place, I would never return to so wretched an abode. Every room is filled with huge heaps of papers, MSS, books, charters, packages and other things, lying in heaps under your feet, piled upon tables, beds, chairs, ladders etc., and in every room, piles of huge boxes, up to the ceiling, containing the more valuable volumes! It is quite sickening! I asked him why he did not clear away the piles of papers etc. from the floor, so as to allow a path to be kept, but he only laughed and said I was not *used to it* as he was! The windows of the house are never opened, and the close confined air and smell of the paper and MSS is almost unbearable.[57]

The Mouse

The mouse is hooked on cheese, but he is always afraid that it might be attached to a trap. He is nervous, torn between desire and fear, continually coming out of his hole to nibble, but, at the slightest noise, darting right back. Eventually he gets caught because in his ignorance he cannot distinguish between the bait and the booty.

I know a mouse to whom one could safely offer a genuine Titian for £10,000, knowing full well he would be far too nervous to take one up on the offer. When, however, he is presented with a totally worthless picture for a few pounds, he will, after much procrastination, eventually swallow the bait and throw his money away.

This particular collector's favourite topic of conversation is about the pictures that got away, especially at auction. The reason that he has acquired nothing in the salerooms turns out to be that he has always been too timorous to bid. Then, after the sale, he kicks himself for not having bid on some lot or other that seemed to have gone to somebody else at a bargain price.

The Roman Knight Mamurra was the collector type of the mouse. Martial has left us this account of his daily visits to the auction places:

[Mammura] spends hours in gadding about, reviews the rows of young slaves which he devours with the eyes of a critic, not, if you please, the common ones but the choicest samples, those that are not on show to everyone...not to common people like us. When he has had enough of this show, he goes to examine the furniture; there he discovers some richly worked round tables hidden beneath some covering; then he orders that some pieces of ivory furniture he wishes to examine be taken down from the highest spot; afterwards he passes on to examine a hexaclinon, a couch used in the triclinium, with six places, veneered with tortoise shell, and measures it four times. What a pity it's not big enough to match his citrus table! A minute later he goes to a small bronze: does it really smell of the Corinthian alloy? Of course he is ready to criticize even your statues, O

Polycletus! Then those two rock crystals are not pure, some are a trifle nebulous, others are marred by slight imperfections. Ah! here's a murrhine. He orders about a dozen to be set aside. He goes to handle some old cups as if he would weigh the merit of each one, more especially that of Mentos. He goes to count the emeralds on a golden vase, and those enormous pearls we see dangling together on the ears of our elegant ladies. Afterwards he goes everywhere on every side for real sardonynx; his speciality is to collect large and rare pieces of jasper. Finally, about the eleventh hour of the day, Mamurra is completely exhausted, he must go home. He buys for less than three farthings two bowls and takes them with him.

The Magpie

The magpie is attracted to what glitters. Literally speaking, of course, pictures do not glitter, their nearest approach being a glistening of the varnish in a just-finished painting. Metaphorically speaking, however, many works of art have an irresistible glitter in the eyes of the magpie collector. This usually consists of a glittering provenance. The longed-for work of art once belonged to some illustrious person: a king, a great statesman, a famous actor or some other person of note. It is as if the magpie believes that by owning something that once belonged to an illustrious name, some of that famous person's lustre will rub off on to them.

Such was the Roman collector Euctus. I follow Riccardo Nobili's neat summary of Martial's satire on this magpie.

Isn't Euctus a bore with his historical silver? ... I would rather eat off the common earthenware of Saguntus than hear all that gabble concerning Euctus's table silver. Think of it! His cups belonged to Laomedon, King of Troy. And, mind, to obtain these rarities Apollo played upon his lyre and destroyed the wall of the city by inducing the stones to follow him by his music. 'Now what do you think of this vase?' asks Euctus of his table companions. 'Well, it belonged to old Nestor himself. Do you see that part all worn away, there where the dove is? It was reduced to that state by the hand of the king of Pylos.' Then, showing one of those mixing bowls that Latins called 'crater': 'This was the cause of the battle between the ferocious Rhoecus and the Lapithae.' Naturally every cup has its particular history. 'This is the very cup used by the sons of Aeacus when offering most generous wine to their friend. That is the cup from which Dido drank to the health of Bythias when she offered him that supper in Phrygia.' Finally, when he had bored his guests to death, Euctus offers them, in the cup from which Pyramus used to drink, 'wine as young as Astyanax'.

At this point the reader may be wondering how the faker approaches such private collectors to sell their pictures. The answer is that if they are wise they do not! This is because whatever form the undesirable collector takes – and there are many more types than have been included in the preceding menagerie – they are all dangerous animals and difficult to handle. You approach their cages at your own risk. They are armed with teeth and claws provided by the law to protect innocent/ignorant people from the dishonest rogues we are assumed to be. Furthermore, although there are collectors who set themselves up as experts and continually discover masterpieces for a song (incidentally these are the easiest prey for the unscrupulous members of our profession) on the whole the collector does not pretend to have great expertise and depends on the judgement of experts and dealers. Consequently, there is about as much satisfaction in selling a picture to somebody who cannot appreciate it as in playing tennis with the net down. Leave the feeding of such animals to the professional purveyors of their food: the dealer. Should it happen that one of these not very knowledgeable collectors escapes his cage and starts prowling around your premises be scrupulously honest with them. Describe your goods accurately and ask an honest price.

Having been rude about certain types of collectors I should now like to speak in praise of the good ones. Not, however, of the very great collectors, whose love and knowledge of art has directly or indirectly so enriched our public collections. Here I have in mind not only the Medicis, the Mellons and the Rothschilds of this world but also such artist–collectors as Vasari, Rembrandt, Reynolds and others, who collected for the love of the art. These enthusiasts and their collections are mostly well known and need no attention in these pages. Instead I would like to introduce two collectors whose names are not generally known. One of modest means, the other prosperous, but both driven by an appreciation of art to use their money to encourage the production of it.

Thomas Butts

In a letter to George Cumberland, the then neglected English genius William Blake writes: 'As to myself, about whom you are so kindly interested, I live by miracle.' That miracle was Thomas Butts, the chief clerk in the Muster-Master-General's Office, whose duty it was to write letters dealing with the enlistment of soldiers. He had commissioned Blake to paint 50 small pictures from the Bible at a time when the artist could not find work even as a reproductive engraver, an art in which he was a highly skilled practitioner.

Butts continued to buy from Blake to the end of the artist's life, and nearly all of Blake's 165 extant illustrations to the Bible come from his collection. He did not buy these works for investment (we would have never dreamed of selling them), he bought them because he recognized Blake's extraordinary gifts. Geoffrey Keynes, the Blake scholar, has described Butts as a 'dumb admirer of genius, which he could see but not quite understand'. What a cheek! What condescension! Well, a dumb admirer is far preferable to a loquacious detractor, and Blake, conscious of his good fortune in meeting with Butts, wrote to his patron:

> Be assured, my dear friend, that there is not one touch in these drawings and pictures but what came from my hand and my heart in unison; that I am proud of being their author and grateful to you, my employer; and that I look upon you as the chief of my friends, whom I would endeavour to please, because you, among all men, have enabled me to produce all these things.[59]

The world could use a few more collectors like Thomas Butts, and then perhaps we would have a few more artists like William Blake.

Luman Reed

Luman Reed was an American trader who, in 1832, gave up his wholesale and retail grocery business in New York. With the fortune he had amassed he built a fine mansion on Greenwich Street and began to collect pictures. At first he collected 'Old Masters' but made the mistake of buying from a dealer whose name, Michael Paff, was, because of his dishonest ways, to become something of a joke. On realizing that he was being cheated, Reed decided to buy the work of contemporary artists. He turned the top storey of his new house into a picture gallery, a novelty in America at the time, and opened it one day a week to the public. In the evenings he would entertain in the gallery artists such as Thomas Cole (1801–48), Asher B. Durand (1796–1886) and William Sidney Mount (1807–68), from whom he bought and commissioned pictures. On being asked by a business acquaintance why he spent so much on art, he replied: 'The outlay is my pleasure. I like it, besides the artists are my friends, and it is a means of encouragement and support to better men than myself.'

Naturally Reed was held in the highest esteem by the artists, and Durand's son wrote of him: '[he was] the first wealthy and intelligent connoisseur who detected and encouraged native ability in other directions than portraiture.' Not only did Reed dip into his pocket to buy pictures but also to finance artists to visit Europe to study. His generosity to the painters he knew is well expressed by the following anecdote. Reed had commissioned a picture from Cole, who on being asked what he wanted for the work had said: 'I shall be satisfied if I receive $300 for it, but I should be gratified if the price is fixed at $500.' Reed replied: 'You shall be gratified.'

When Reed died in the early 1840s, his many friends, in the fields of both art and business, clubbed together to buy his collection and founded an institute called the New York Gallery of Fine Arts. This was intended to be a permanent monument to him. But due to public indifference no suitable building was offered to house the collection, and Reed's actual monument lies today in the individual works of art that, without his patronage, might never have come into existence.

Would that collectors of Mr Butts' and Mr Reed's calibre were more in evidence today. Doubtless they still exist but have been so brow-beaten by intellectual snobs, critics and purveyors of modern art that, understandably enough, these wonderful people stifle the urge to follow their own judgement.

It has been the purpose of this chapter to give profiles of certain types of private collectors whom one may come across and to suggest that you do not offer your fakes to them unless they are acting on 'expert advice'. The reason for not selling to them directly is that they are, generally speaking, not knowledgeable enough to decide for themselves what it is they are buying. To take advantage of their ignorance is not only unfair and gives no satisfaction but also, as we shall see in the following chapter, if you make a false warranty you are not just being naughty you are being totally crooked as well.

CHAPTER FOURTEEN

A Brush with the Law

'A jury consists of twelve persons chosen to decide who has the
better lawyer.'
ROBERT FROST

In England in 1562 the forging of a signature was punishable by being
pilloried, having one's ears cut off, one's nose slit up, one's land forfeited
and life imprisonment. Nor were matters to get any better for the forger,
for after 1634 the penalty was death. One person executed for his penmanship
was the Reverend Dr W. Dodd, convicted of forging Lord Chesterfield's
signature on a bond.

By English law today the actual making of a fake drawing or painting is
not illegal. It is only when an attempt is made to sell it as an original that a
crime has been committed, that of deliberate fraud. The criminal is convicted
of having gained pecuniary advantage by false pretences and may justly be
jailed for it.

To establish that deliberate fraud has, in fact, been perpetrated, the prosecution normally begins by attempting to show that the new 'Old Master'
has been executed in old materials. This is not in itself sufficient evidence to
demonstrate that the artist was setting out from the very beginning to
deceive. This is because many impoverished painters paint their pictures on
old boards and canvases picked up cheaply in junk shops or flea markets and
many draughtsmen and etchers prefer old hand-made paper to the modern
machine-made variety. Whistler (1834–1903), for example, frequently
printed his etchings on old paper. Nevertheless, if the work in question has
been drawn or painted on an old support with 'old' materials, in the style of
a former age, and artificially aged, it does tend to point in a certain direction.

And if the work bears a forged signature then, although not conclusive, things do begin to look bad even for the most innocent practitioner of our art. What clinches the matter in favour of the prosecution, however, is if it can be shown that the work was sold by the forger for a price that it could not have fetched unless it had been offered as an original creation of the master named. In short, the swindle consists in wrongly describing an object in order to obtain a sum of money for it that is grossly in excess of its market value. For this reason the law-abiding forger will make no warranty, and above all he will ask a fair price for his handiwork. It is on this last point that his case rests, and it cannot be stressed too much: DO NOT BE GREEDY.

Nobody expects you to work for nothing, but to ask £100,000 for a picture that is only worth £1000 is clearly cheating, and you deserve to be punished for it.

The solution to this problem is to ask the same price for your fakes as for work signed with your own name. Clearly if you are not an artist with an established reputation and quotation you will have to find another way for pricing your fakes. I would suggest you do it on the basis of the time you have spent in their making. Charge the price per hour that any skilled worker, let us say a plumber, would expect to be paid for the time involved and add to this the cost of your materials. You may now sell your fakes with a clear conscience, knowing that although they may lead your customer into thinking they have bought a great bargain and cheated you out of a valuable possession, you are not guilty of having swindled them.

Forging Certificates of Authentification

Under this heading one word should suffice: DON'T! The forging of these documents involves the very serious crime of making a false warranty with clear intent to defraud.

The Case of J. S. G. Boggs

In October 1986 at the private view of an exhibition at the Young Unknowns Gallery in London, the works of the American painter J. S. G. Boggs were seized by the police. This was not because of them being fake pictures, but because they were suspected of being fake banknotes. What the artist had done was to make drawings of one £10 note, one £5 note, and two £1 notes. These drawings were made with crayons, were one-sided and carried the signature of the artist. Notwithstanding, the police suspected Boggs of having contravened Section 18 of the 1981 Forgery and Counterfeiting Act. In the event it was not the police who prosecuted the artist but the Bank of England, and the case came to court at the Old Bailey in November 1987.

Boggs' lawyer argued that his client's 'banknotes' were so different from the real ones that 'not even a moron in a hurry' could be deceived by them. Three well-known figures in the art world were called in to testify: Michael Compton (formerly of the Tate Gallery), the dealer René Gimpel, and the director of Visual Arts at the Arts Council, Sandy Nairne. These authorities all agreed on one point: it would be quite incorrect to describe an artist's drawing of an object as a reproduction of it. An artist who draws, for example, a tree is clearly not guilty of having faked a tree. From which it follows that if we make a drawing of an engraving (which a banknote is), a painting or a piece of sculpture, we cannot be accused of having faked an engraving, painting or piece of sculpture. Our drawings are, for better or for worse, original drawings. Should anybody subsequently deceive themselves into thinking that they are not after the works of art we have drawn, but preparatory studies for such works, that is no concern of ours or the law's.

Obviously Mr Boggs wanted to raise questions other than legal ones: he is a conceptual artist, and his drawings are intended to make us think. Not to wonder about whether or not we like them aesthetically but about our basic assumptions regarding the value of both money and art. To get our thought processes oiled, Boggs offers his drawings at the face value of the banknote represented. Even though it is plain enough that it takes no more time or skill to draw a £10 note than it does a £5 one, his £10 note is valued at £10 and his £5 note at £5 and so on. The artist does not, however, simply sell his drawings but also uses them as currency by persuading collectors to swap goods to the value of the note represented. The fruit of these transactions are then exhibited in the gallery in place of the drawn work.

Put very simply, what Mr Boggs is pointing out is something we all know, but which many of us are reluctant to admit: in our society art is equated with money. What counts about a picture is not its aesthetic merit but its market value. In this it is exactly like a banknote. In so far as the note is an engraving, designed by an artist, it is a work of art – a very popular work of art. But it is not its artistic value that makes a £20 note twice as attractive as a £10 note and not half as attractive as a £50 one.

The obvious difference between a banknote and other engraved, drawn or painted works of art lies in it being a legal document. It makes a legally binding verbal promise to pay the bearer a certain sum of money on presentation to the issuing bank. A picture, on the other hand, makes no promises. It does not promise to be worth money, to be beautiful, to be old or new, by this or that artist, genuine or spurious. As far as the law is concerned it makes no warranty whatsoever. This being so, any signature appended to it does not involve the owner of that name in any legally binding obligations. Had the unfortunate Reverend Dr W. Dodd put Lord Chesterfield's signature on a painting instead of a bond, it is unlikely, even in those rough times, that he would have been charged, let alone executed.

Similarly Mr Boggs only got into trouble because he had imitated a legal document closely enough conceivably to pose a threat to public interest. In the event common sense prevailed, and the artist was acquitted. To have been charged at all shows what a sensitive area Boggs had touched. So sensitive, in fact, that in 1989 he was again threatened with legal action, this time in Australia. Since then he has had several brushes with the law.

To sum up this brief note on fakers and the law:

1. The making of a new Old Master is not in itself a crime.
2. A crime has only been committed when the fake is offered for sale as a genuinely old picture.
3. The price asked for the picture will be taken as testimony as to what claims the vendor was making for the work.
4. The faking of Certificates of Authentication is very definitely illegal.

Apart from a few notes, with no pretence whatsoever to being proper, scholarly apparatus, this brings my book to an end. I trust the reader has found something of interest in its pages and wish them every success in the gentle art of faking pictures. Should some little difference arise between you and your customers, console yourself with the words of the novelist and critic Dame Rebecca West: 'Any authentic work of art must start an argument between the artist and his audience.' Just try and settle out of court.

Notes

1 Walter Richard Sickert: *A Free House* (London, 1947, p.xxxi).

2 Ibid.

3 Max Doerner: *The Materials of the Artist & their Use in Painting* (London, 1960, p.vii).

4 Cited by Sepp Schüller in *Forgers, Dealers and Experts* (London, 1960, p.xv).

5 Baldassare Castiglione: *Il cortegiano* (Milan, 1991; first published 1518).

6 Cennino Cennini: *Il libro dell'arte* (Florence, c.1390; with a commentary and note by F. Brunello, Venice, 1982; trans. Daniel V. Thompson as *The Craftsman's Handbook*, 1933).

7 Werner Muensterberger: *Collecting: An Unruly Passion* (Princeton, 1994, p.37).

8 Tom Keating, Geraldine Norman and Frank Norman: *The Fake's Progress* (London, 1977, p.84).

9 John Evelyn: *The Diary of John Evelyn* (London, 1959, p.2).

10 Edward Johnston: *Writing & Illuminating & Lettering* (London, 1906).

11 Giorgio Vasari: *Le vite dei più eccellenti pittori, scultori e architetti* (1550, enlarged edn 1568; ed. C. Ragghianti, 4 vols, Milan, 1942, vol. 2, pp.241–2).

12 Cennini, op. cit., pp.17–19.

13 Ibid., p.9.

14 A.J. Pernety: *Dictionnaire de peinture, sculpture et gravure* (Paris, 1775).

15 Michelangelo Buonarroti: *Rime* (ed. Ettore Barelli, Milan, 1975, p.139).

16 Vasari, op. cit., vol. 3, p.404.

17 H.J. Plenderleith: *The Conservation of Antiquities and Works of Art* (London, p.84).

18 Keating et al., op. cit., p.84.

19 This comes from an article by Otto Kurz in *Old Master Drawings*, xii, 1937, pp.1ff and pp.32ff.

20 Ibid.

21 A.E. Popham: 'Sebastiano Resta and his Collections', *Old Master Drawings*, xi, 1937, pp.1ff.

22 *Cento tavole del Codice Resta* (Milan, 1955).

23 Cennini, op. cit., p.15.

24 Vergnand Riffault: *Nouveau manuel complet du peintre* (Paris, 1843).

25 Hilaire Hiler: *Notes on the Technique of Painting* (London, 1934, p.49).

26 J. G. Vibert: *La Science de la Peinture* (Paris, 1891, p.170).

27 Cennini, op. cit., p.111.

28 Mark Jones, ed.: *Fake?* (London, 1990, p.235).

29 Hiler, op. cit., p.32.

30 Vasari, op. cit., Introduction, p.163.

31 Ibid., p.236.

32 Hiler, op. cit., p.60.

33 Cennini, op. cit., p.44.

34 Maurice Busset: *La technique moderne du tableau et les procédés des grands coloristes des XV–XVII siècles* (Paris, 1929).

35 A. P. Laurie: *Materials of the Painters' Craft* (London, 1910, pp.46–7).

36 T. De Mayerne: 'Pictoria, sculptoria, tinctoria et quae subalternarum artium', *Beitrage zur Entwicklungsgeschichte der Maltechnik*, E. Berger (IV, Munich, 1901, vol. xxvi, 1876).

37 Cennini, op. cit., p.40.

38 Ibid., p.69.

39 R. Spencer Stanhope: *Papers of the Society of British Tempera Painters* (vol. 1, p.41).

40 Hiler, op. cit., p.176.

41 Ibid.

42 Philippe Nuñez: *Arte da Pintura* (Lisbon, 1615).

43 Doerner, op. cit., p.145.

44 Hiler, op. cit., p.255.

45 Walter Thornbury: *The Life of J. M. W. Turner, RA* (2 vols, London, 1862, vol. 1, p.262).

46 Sarah Symmons, 'John Flaxman and Francisco Goya: Inferno Transcribed', *Burlington Magazine*, cxiii, 822, p.508.

47 Ibid.

48 Eric Hebborn: *Drawn to Trouble: The Forging of an Artist, an Autobiography* (Edinburgh, 1991), p.153.

49 W. R. Rearick, 'Jacopo Bassano's Later Genre Painting', *Burlington Magazine*, cx, 782, May 1968.

50 Hebborn, op. cit., p.117.

51 Hiler, op. cit., p.286.

52 Frederick Hartt: *The Drawings of Michelangelo* (London, 1971, p.245).

53 A. P. Laurie: *New Light on Old Masters* (London, 1935, p.142).

54 Ibid., p.144.

55 Alan Clark: *Diaries* (London, 1993, p.228).

56 Russell Lynes: *The Taste Makers* (New York, 1954, pp.45–7).

57 Ibid.

58 Sir Frederick Madden: *Diary* (Bodleian Library, Oxford).

59 Geoffrey Keynes: *The Complete Writings of William Blake* (London, 1966, pp.814–15).

The Forger's Bookshelf

Because this book does not try to be an erudite text, it does not seem to me to be necessary to include an exhaustive bibliography of my sources. The reader will find in the text and notes the references to the texts that I have mainly used. There are a great number of books that the interested reader will find amusing, useful and essential while studying this subject in greater depth.

The material that gives the forger the necessary knowledge to deceive the experts is given by books on materials and painters' methods, books on history in general and on art history in particular, on costume, mythology, religion, restoration, architecture, heraldry, catalogues and specialized publications, and books with good reproductions, especially in the field of prints. These are texts that can be found in a good public library.

However, there are three titles that the forger should have at his disposal for reference at any time.

E. Bénézit: *Dictionnaire des peintres, sculpteurs, dessinateurs et graveurs*, 10 vols, Librairie Gründ, France, 1960.
C. M. Briques: *Les Filigranes*, 4 vols, Hacker Art Books.
F. Lugt: *Les Marques de Collections de dessins et d'estampes*, 2 vols, 1st edn, Martinus Nijhoff, Amsterdam, 1921.

These are the basic instruments for the serious student, and if you are able to afford to buy them (they are very expensive), it will be money well spent. Used judiciously, they will pay for themselves.

Photographic
Acknowledgements

Plates 1–2: Archeus Fine Art, London; **Plate 3:** Statens Museum for Kunst, Copenhagen; **Plate 4:** Archeus Fine Art, London; **Plate 5:** Sotheby's, London; **Plates 6–8:** Archeus Fine Art, London; **Plate 9:** private collection/Bridgeman Art Library, London; **Plate 10:** Fitzwilliam Museum, Cambridge/Bridgeman Art Library, London; **Plate 11:** Archeus Fine Art, London; **Plate 12:** Graphische Sammlung Albertina, Vienna; **Plate 13:** private collection, Switzerland; **Plate 14:** private collection, Austria; **Plate 15:** private collection, London; **Plate 16:** British Museum, London; **Plate 17:** Archeus Fine Art, London; **Plate 18:** Ashmolean Museum, Oxford; **Plate 19:** Nasjonalgalleriet, Oslo; **Plate 20:** Pierpont Morgan Library, New York, I, 191; **Plates 21–2:** Archeus Fine Art, London; **Plate 23:** The Royal Collection © Her Majesty The Queen; **Plate 24:** National Museum, Krakow; **Plate 25:** Archeus Fine Art, London; **Plate 26:** Teylers Museum, Haarlem; **Plate 27:** Archeus Fine Art, London; **Plate 28:** Museum voor Schone Kunsten/Musée des Beaux-Arts, Antwerp; **Plates 29–30:** National Gallery, London; **Plates 31–2:** Christie's Images, London; **Plate 33:** Archeus Fine Art, London; **Plate 34:** National Gallery, London; **Plate 36:** Biblioteca Nacional, Madrid; **Plate 37:** Kathedraal van Onze-Lieve-Vrouw, Antwerp; **Plate 38:** Museum Boymans-van Beuningen, Rotterdam; **Plates 39–40:** Archeus Fine Art, London; **Plate 41:** Fototeca e Archivi Alinari, Florence; **Plate 42:** Museo Poldi-Pezzoli, Milan; **Plates 43–8:** Ben Gooder, London; **Plate 49:** Museo del Prado, Madrid; **Plates 50-3:** National Gallery, London.

pp. 64–7 and p. 69: E. Bénézit, *Dictionnaire des peintres, sculpteurs, dessinateurs et graveurs*, 8 vols., Librairie Gründ, Paris, 1960; pp. 71–2: F. Lugt, *Les Marques de Collections de dessins et d'estampes*, 2 vols. Martinus Nijhoff, Amsterdam, 1921; p. 127: Museo Civico, Bassano del Grappa; p. 128: Pinacoteca Ambrosiana, Milan; p. 129: Fototeca e Archivi Alinari, Florence; p. 130: Museo Civico, Bassano del Grappa; pp. 142–5: KIK-IRPA, Brussels.

Line drawings: Archeus Fine Art, London.

Index